D1565815

Hidden Presence

Twelve Blessings That Transformed Sorrow or Loss

Gregory F. Augustine Pierce, Ed.

ASSISTING CHRISTIANS TO ACT

PUBLICATIONS

Hidden Presence
Twelve Blessings That Transformed Sorrow or Loss
Edited by Gregory F. Augustine Pierce

Cover design and photo by Tom A. Wright
Typesetting by Desktop Edit Shop, Inc.

Copyright © 2003 by ACTA Publications

Published by: ACTA Publications
                Assisting Christians To Act
                4848 N. Clark Street
                Chicago, IL 60640-4711
                773-271-1030
                www.actapublications.com

Library of Congress Catalog Number: 2003109366
ISBN: 0-87946-252-3
Printed in the United States of America
Year: 08 07 06 05 04 03 02
Printing: 10 9 8 7 6 5 4 3 2 1

Contents

Dedication

To Father Gerard Weber,
a great Chicago priest and educator,
who taught us about the Paschal Mystery...
and lived as if he believed it
every day of his life.

Introduction

Bad things happen. They happen to good people. They happen to all of us and to our friends and loved ones.

Are these tragedies, disasters, sorrows and losses somehow a punishment for our sins—real or imagined, original or actual, mortal or venial? Jesus pretty much put that idea to rest when he cured the man born blind. "Who has sinned, this man or his parents?" the Pharisees asked. "Neither," Jesus answered, implying that it was entirely the wrong question to ask. "If you were blind, you would not have sin," he told them. "But now that you say, 'We see,' your sin remains."

But still, bad things do happen. Even very good people (as far as we can determine, anyway) get sick, face financial ruin, are caught in earthquakes, hurricanes and fires. They lose loved ones—to death, to drugs, to anger, to indifference. They are hurt, saddened, disappointed on a regular basis. This is what we abstractly and much too clinically refer to as "the human condition," as if our sorrows and losses are somehow not the kick in the groin they feel like.

Perhaps the first step in dealing with the bad things that happen to us is to admit that they are bad. Nor are they going to become good just because we try to get over them or time manages to heal some of the wounds or we start to get on with life or we pray about them or learn to accept them. No, bad things are bad, and they remain bad, even when they happen to good people.

But there is another truth that we also must admit, and that is that sometimes—not all the time, but some of the time—bad things lead to good things. These good things—let us call them "blessings"—do not make the bad things any less bad. Nor do the good things make us glad that the bad things happened. It's just that somehow, in ways we don't understand and can't even imagine, sorrow or loss are transformed by blessings we neither seek nor expect. Something truly good occurs, not *despite* the bad thing but actually *because* the bad thing occurred (even though we still wish it never had).

I experienced one such blessing, in the person of my father, that transformed a great sorrow and loss in my life.

—

The worst period in my life occurred right after I was divorced for the second time in the early 1980s, when I was in my mid-thirties. I felt I was a "two-time loser," a failure at what seemed to be the most natural and vital of all human relationships. I was sure that I would never have the children I wanted so badly, convinced that there was something seriously wrong with me.

My living arrangements reflected my self-image. I had rented a little one-and-a-half room apartment in Brooklyn. It was a crummy place, one of several apartments squeezed into a former single-family house on Third Street and Seventh Avenue in the Park Slope neighborhood, which was being regentrified at the time. But my building had definitely not yet been redone. The apartment was dark, there were plenty of cockroaches, and the bathroom out in the hall—with tub but no shower—was shared with the other tenants (with none of us assigned the job of cleaning it).

Early one Saturday morning, as I was walking out the front door of the old brownstone building, I felt a bug of some kind in my hair. However, I looked up and noticed that it wasn't a bug at all. Instead, some kind of dust was falling from the door jamb. At exactly the same time, two men who were standing on the sidewalk in front of the building drinking coffee yelled, "Look out!" I looked up again and realized that the stone overhang over the entrance was rapidly on its way toward me. I had no time to think but reacted by pressing myself face-first against the front door, which had just closed behind me. The stones fell in what seemed slow motion—not directly down but more like a column would topple. Huge chunks of Brooklyn brownstone smashed down the concrete stairs directly behind me.

In a couple of seconds, it was over. "Jesus," the men said as they ran over. "How did you survive that? Look at the size of those rocks! Any one of them could have killed you."

I admitted that I did not know how I had survived, but I shared in their invocation of the Lord. I was shaken up, no doubt about it. But there was nothing to be done. "I'm going to get a cup of coffee," I told the men.

"You oughta buy a lottery ticket, too," one of them said.

When I returned a few minutes later, the men were gone.

I picked up one of the smaller pieces of brownstone—one of the few I could even lift—and went in to call the landlord and tell him what had happened. I still have that rock with me today.

—

A few months later, my parents came to visit me from Rochester, New York. They absolutely hated New York City, in a way only lifelong upstaters can, but they came anyway to be with their prodigal son. I tried to put the best face on my life, but once they took a look at my living quarters they realized how badly I was hurting.

That Sunday, my father announced that he and I were going to look for a new apartment for me. My father and I had never had that kind of relationship. I was the oldest son, had left home when I was seventeen to go to college, and had always been independent. In fact, both Dad and I had always acted as if I knew exactly what I was doing and that there was nothing much he could or should do for me. If anything, I would have expected Mom to offer to help me find a new apartment, not Dad.

But he was insistent and not to be otherwise persuaded, so after church that morning he and I walked up and down the streets of Park Slope. There were plenty of apartments for rent, and quite a few buildings had been made into condos and co-ops that were for sale. But all were clearly out of my post-divorce price range. But for some reason, Dad did not give up. Usually, he is an impatient man. If things do not go his way right away, he tends to lose interest. But not that day. We kept going, looking at apartment after apartment and finding nothing.

After several hours, we found ourselves almost back at our starting place. In fact, we were on Fourth Street and Seventh Avenue, just one block away from the dive I was living in. There was a sign in the building on the corner that said there was a co-op apartment for sale. "Let's skip it, Dad," I said. "I don't want to buy into a co-op, and I can't afford anything in this neighborhood anyway."

I remember him gently pushing me into the building. "This will be the last one, Greg. Let's just look."

The apartment turned out to be a fourth-floor walkup, which was not an easy climb for my father, who had been out of shape for many years. But he climbed the stairs with me, and we discovered a wonderful, airy two-bedroom apartment that had been totally rebuilt. Everything in it was fresh and clean. It had beautiful hardwood floors, new appliances, and lots of windows and light. I actually liked it, but I said, "Let's go, Dad. I could never afford this place."

The salesman said, "By the way, since this is the top floor, you get exclusive rights to the roof."

So Dad and I went back out into the hallway and trudged up one more flight of stairs. There was a door that opened to the flat roof, and we walked out onto it. The view took our breath away. Park Slope is so named because it slopes up from the East River, and this building was on one of the highest points in Brooklyn. Plus we were on the fifth floor with no high buildings blocking the view. To the west was the entire skyline of Manhattan, looking as if we could reach out and touch it. To the south was the New York harbor, with the Verrazano Bridge and the Statue of Liberty clearly visible.

"This is where you should be living, Greg," Dad told me.

"I don't even have the money for the down payment," I told him plaintively.

"Yes, you do," he said. He proceeded to tell me that the money I had invested a few years earlier in the bookstore he and my mother had started had grown to about $8000. He would make it available if I wanted to buy the place.

—

And that's exactly what happened. I bought the apartment, moved in, and began to feel better about myself. A year or so later, I met a teacher in a Catholic school in Chicago. We began dating, and eventually I invited her to visit me in Brooklyn. When she observed me in my nice environment (and especially when she discovered the romantic view from the roof), she apparently concluded that I was not a "loser." We eventually married and now live in Chicago with our three teenage children.

Oh, yeah. We sold the co-op in Brooklyn for almost double what I had paid for it.

And my relationship with my Dad has been different ever since that Sunday morning.

And the chunk of brownstone still sits outside the front door of our home.

—

Kathy and I ended up in Chicago, where I became a writer, editor and publisher. I began to wonder if others had ever had a similar experience of bad things—large or small—that had led somehow to good things in their lives, and I discovered that many had. So I asked a dozen of my favorite spiritual writers to share a story of a blessing they had received that had transformed a sorrow or loss in their own life. These are their stories:

- **Terry Nelson-Johnson** painted a picture of his Uncle Bob, a Jesuit priest who has been a hero and mentor to him throughout his life but is now "shrinking" before his eyes. "My uncle is walking into the sacred space of not knowing, the sacred space of vulnerability and weakness, the sacred space of dying," he explains. "He is *expecting* to arrive, *expecting* new life. Bob is living the Paschal Mystery and allowing me to sit at his swollen feet (preferably while massaging them) while he does so."

- **Helen Reichert Lambin** spent thirty years married to her best friend, Henry. When he died she "did what prisoners have done from time immemorial: divided the time I had left into what seemed more manageable blocks—360 months to be exact." She then proceeded to try to live her life with the idea that each month was only 1/360th of the time she had spent with her husband. She is now at six years and counting, and has learned that "time, which had seemed a prison to be endured, had become a gift—and a responsibility—to be used as well as possible. I learned that there was much more to this than simply filling in all those blank squares of months, or days, or years. It was what you fill them with."

- **Kass Dotterweich** recalled how an unexpected (and unwanted) pregnancy when her husband was on strike from his job led to a reconciliation both with her church and with God that prepared her heart to make room for her sixth child. "Never since have I entertained my own prideful, self-serving and self-righteous anger to the point of feeling beyond God's unbound beneficence," she writes.

- **Patrick Hannon** confessed that "the first thing you need to know is that I never asked to come to Chicago." He then proceeded to tell the story of how a serious bout with depression led to a connection with one of his students and the boy's mother. "I was told once, or maybe I read it somewhere," he writes, "that despair is not the end of hope. It is the beginning of hope. It is one of those seemingly unbelievable paradoxes of our faith that it doesn't so much explain suffering as allow us to live through it."

- **Robert Raccuglia** told how a heart attack at the age of forty-three and the subsequent breakdown of his marriage had forced him to come to grips with who he really is. "If it was hard for me to give up the illusion of myself as a perfectly healthy person when the heart problems arose," he explains, "it was devastating for me to let go of my self perception as a perfectly good husband and father when I got divorced."

- **Alice Camille** wrote about how she has been ambushed by failure in several forms, only to discover that it taught her many important life lessons. "Finally, after all these years," she says, "I was learning how to know what I knew. I knew that failure, the shadowy enemy that had tracked my footsteps for years, was an ally."

- **Vinita Hampton Wright** revealed the story of her miscarriage. "I want to describe some changes that have happened as a result of the miscarriage," she explains. "The loss has somehow added to my fullness as a person. My life is now, oddly enough, larger than it was before this grief."

- **Patrick Reardon** admitted that if it weren't for his congenital aversion to wasting money, he never would have met his wife, had his kids, or become the successful newspaper writer he has become: "Suddenly, at age thirty-one, after a lifetime of robust good health, I was sick—and not just sick but ill with a mystery ailment that had my doctor flummoxed. I had no energy. I felt overwhelmed, crushed."

- **James (Jeff) Behrens** returned to the scene of the car crash that took the life of his twin brother and found there his common humanity with others who mourn the loss of a loved one. "Our lives and loves will rise," he insists. "A fullness awaits us all. Meanwhile, we have roads to walk and comfort to give to those who are hurting."

- **Joyce Rupp** recalled the death of her brother in a drowning accident years ago and how her grief had forced her to travel within herself. "Grieving the devastating loss of Dave's death gave me the blessing of learning how to live with myself," she writes. "It gave me confidence to enter my inner terrain. It is a blessing that continues to influence me every day of my life. I never wanted my brother to die, nor would I ever have chosen this path to come to self-revelation and growth. But it was the gift that Dave gave to me, and I would be ungrateful indeed if I did not treasure it."

- **Joni Woelfel** lived through the worst nightmare a parent can imagine: the suicide of her child. "I know my journey is nothing short of extraordinary," she reflects. "I can't wrap my mind around it and don't try to. Instead, my life's mission is to live simply and mindfully one day at a time and be an authentic spiritual voice of comfort and insight as much as I can."

- Finally, **Michael Leach** shared how a childhood accident to his wife's eye, the loss of a job in Ohio, and the deaths of one friend and one mentor had all made him rediscover "that God's grace connects every dot, every fall, every rising."

All of these stories by these accomplished writers reveal the divine love that is present at all times in our lives, even when things seem the darkest. This presence is often hidden, but if we are open to it and looking for it, we will discover it.

Or, more likely, God's blessings will find us when we are least expecting them.

The Shrinking Jesuit (in Shiny New "Chick Magnet" Scooter) Leads the Way

by Terry Nelson-Johnson

ne of my earliest memories is that of being bundled as a little boy of five or six into a car with some other members of my family to make the trek from Chicago to Milwaukee. Unbeknownst to me, we were going to watch my Uncle Bob, a Jesuit priest, perform in the play *Green Pastures* on the campus of Marquette University.

I have no memory of the story line of the play, but I will never forget Uncle Bob, who played the Lord, and his African-American sidekick, the angel Gabriel. For whatever reason (although as a five-year-old boy it made perfect sense to me), Gabriel was eager to blow his trumpet but needed permission from my uncle—the Lord. Periodically over the course of the play Gabriel, trumpet poised at his lips, would make an impassioned, baritoned plea to Uncle Bob: "Now, Lord?" In the wake of each request, Bob responded compassionately but firmly, "Not yet, Gabe."

As far as I was concerned, the rest of the play was pretty slow, but the trumpet-request dialogue was high drama. While I was enjoying the Lord's poise and steadfastness and benevolent exercise of power, I sure hoped he would relent and let Gabriel have at it before I succumbed to sleep. It was already way past my bedtime when sure enough, just before I lost consciousness, I heard Gabriel plaintively seek trumpet permission once again. This time, Uncle Bob turned to Gabriel and smiled a deep smile. As I drifted off to sleep, I knew that this was it. The Lord—my uncle—spread his arms wide and proclaimed (as Lords are want to do): "Now, Gabe! Blow!" And Gabriel blew.

I took into my youthful ears the powerful and haunting and delightful sound of the trumpet, and I took into my heart my uncle.

I took into my youthful ears the powerful and haunting and delightful sound of the trumpet, and I took into my heart my uncle. On that night, at that moment, Bob's presence, person and spirit seemed to fill the stage. He was big; I was little; and we were connected in some enduring and significant way.

Certainly five year olds (or any year olds for that matter) don't decide these kind of things in one evening, but on some level, while beholding my thespian Jesuit uncle fill up the stage during that production of *Green Pastures*, I decided that my Uncle Bob would be my hero, my mentor in the spirit, my confessor and confidant, the guy I would follow through life. Forever after, he would be big and I would be small. And that's the way it was.

Twenty-five years later, I returned with my family to Milwaukee to join in celebrating Father Bob's tenure as Pastor of Gesu Church, an urban Jesuit parish affiliated with Marquette University. When Uncle Bob had arrived, the parish was in simultaneous need of a hospice caretaker and a midwife. My uncle proved a worthy practitioner of both roles. Bob had helped his brother Jesuits and his parishioners let go of that which was no longer life giving and risk new ways of being and doing church that proved to be fruitful and creative. By the time we gathered to celebrate his decade of leadership, the parish was diverse, vital and thriving. Upon walking into the celebration, you could feel the pulse of the place and her people and sense the intimate connection between that pulse and the pastor, Uncle Bob.

At some point in the course of the celebration, Father Bob strode to the center of the sanctuary, spread his arms wide and laughed. The laughter came from some deep, abiding place within him. It was big, like Bob was big. His person, his laughter, his spirit filled the sanctuary. The poetry and choreography of the moment were not lost on my thirty-year-old self. This was the same experience (minus Gabriel and his trumpet) that I had taken in twenty-five years earlier in this same city, the same experience that had connected me to my uncle in some mystical, mysterious, enduring and grace-filled fashion.

As I beheld my mentor in the sanctuary, I marveled at the

wise decision my five-year-old self had made during the dramatic climax of *Green Pastures*. The man in the sanctuary had indeed become my sanctuary. My hero was a large hero.

At innumerable junctures in my life, my uncle ably filled the various roles that I had assigned to him:

- Tears etched on his face, cupping my face in his big hands, he helped me say good-bye to my grandmother, his mom.
- He smelled the grief that eluded others and saw me through the premature ending of my athletic career. (Don't all boys think that their athletic careers end prematurely?)
- He called me a theologian before it was warranted and before it would have occurred to anyone else, including me.
- He listened to my stories as only a storyteller can.
- When I fell in love with a beautiful woman who had a soft spot in her heart for a dreamer, he fell in love with her too. He stood with us in the sanctuary as he witnessed and celebrated our wedding and continued to witness and celebrate our marriage.
- He baptized our children, spreading his arms out wide and welcoming them into life, into the church, into the adventure.

Fifteen years after the Gesu Church celebration, I was standing in another sanctuary with my Uncle Bob. This sanctuary was much smaller than those he had previously filled with such power and grace. Bob was also much smaller. He and I were facing seventy-five family members who had gathered for a Johnson family reunion. Despite his eighty-two years, he had been automatically and respectfully assigned the task of celebrating Mass, and I was to function as the altar boy. As I stood next to him, more or less prepared for liturgy to begin, it struck me that I'd just about had it with the decline of my mentor, my hero, my Uncle Bob.

> All my life, I said that I would follow Bob anywhere, but apparently that did not include accompanying him to the commode.

There had been nothing particularly dramatic or unusual about his diminishment, his shrinking, his getting old. His world had merely gotten progressively smaller. He now needed incrementally increasing assistance to walk, to dress, to eat, to think. I, of all people, should have been the first to step up and afford all the assistance I could muster, but that was not part of the decision I had made upon the blowing of Gabriel's trumpet on that stage in Milwaukee.

All my life, I said that I would follow Bob anywhere, but apparently that did not include accompanying him to the commode. There was something terribly wrong with this picture. Heroes were supposed to go out dramatically. They were not supposed to diminish and shrink. Like my athletic career, my relationship with Uncle Bob was ending prematurely, and who was going to be there to accompany me in my grief?

Given Bob's relatively delicate condition, combined with my very rusty acolyte skills, I had many misgivings about this particular family reunion Mass. As it turned out, these misgivings were well founded. Shortly after we commenced, the Mass began to resemble a New York cab ride gone bad. "Haven't we already said the Our Father twice?" "Isn't the kiss of peace after the readings?" "Which reading is this supposed to be?" For all my familiarity with liturgy from outside the sanctuary, I was unable to be of much assistance to my uncle inside the sanctuary. After all, this was his territory, not mine.

The entire Johnson family was privy to Uncle Bob's unintended dance of diminishment. You know how when you discover someone you care for in a compromised situation you look away in order to afford him time to regain his dignity? Well, suffice it to say that there was a fair amount of looking away going on that day, except for the two strangers who had found out there was a Mass in the chapel and had asked to join us as guests. In lieu of turning away from Bob's embarrassment, the two of them slowly, simultaneously shook their heads, as in, "Isn't this too bad; what a shame!"

Something about the head shaking triggered something in me. First I wanted to throttle the strangers by their simultaneous necks: "Don't you dare shake your heads at my uncle! In his day he was my hero. He filled the stage, the sanctuary, the soul. He was big and brilliant and passionate. He is not to be pitied. He is just…shrinking."

Then I wanted to throttle my mentor: "Snap out of it, Uncle Bob! Come on, this is shameful. Either die or be who I need you to be. No more lingering, no more diminishment."

Finally, I wanted to throttle myself: "Grow up, Terry! Let him go. Your hero needs you now. Care for him, hold him, accompany him in his decline."

So much throttling can wear a fellow out, especially when underneath the throttle is repressed sadness and grief. By the time our family liturgy mercifully ended I was as exhausted as my uncle. I cleaned up the sanctuary after the man who had been my sanctuary, and then I commenced to put my very human uncle to bed for his nap.

Bob's feet are often very swollen and dry these days. When I get the opportunity, I massage them with cream. I was doing this one day when my uncle suggested that he read some of his poetry to me. Truth be told, I'd about had my fill of his meandering musings, but how could I refuse my former mentor? He read the following poem to me, and it changed my life:

Not Knowing

In my life's journey
I have come so far in knowing
Done so much in knowing
Become so much from knowing.

Am I prepared
Ready now
To enter the sacred space of
Not knowing
Not Knowing?

Do I have trust
That such a way
Will bring me to
Arrival?

Robert Purcell, S.J.

When Jesus asked the Pharisees, "Do you have eyes but not see?" I don't think he was using his nice voice. Until Uncle Bob read me his poem, I did not have the eyes to see my hero's negotiation of his diminishment as the most recent, most eloquent exercise of his 'Lordship' in my life. I was stunned by the poem. I still carry it with me every day.

I now see that with his arms open wide, just like on the stage and in the sanctuary, my uncle is walking into the sacred space of not knowing, the sacred space of vulnerability and weakness, the sacred space of dying. He is *expecting* to arrive, *expecting* new life. Bob is living the Paschal Mystery and allowing me to sit at his swollen feet (preferably while massaging them) while he does so.

My uncle's courageous walk into the sacred space of not knowing has proven to be an ironic, challenging and precious gift in my life. The poem has freed me and compelled me to walk into my own sacred spaces of not knowing, in the hopes that such a journey will bring me to arrival.

I come from a home where alcohol was "a factor." Collectively, my siblings and I learned to avoid conflict, to detour around conflict, to finesse conflict. Years after leaving that home, conflict remains a space of not knowing for me. Most often conflict, especially with my loved ones, does not feel sacred, but with Father Bob's poem in hand I am more willing to go there now when my life circumstances ask this of me.

I have been married for twenty years to that beautiful woman who found room in her heart for this dreamer. You would think that there would be no more spaces of not knowing between us. Hardly. In light of my uncle's poem, I have come to appreciate that one of the most profound gestures of love that I can afford my wife is to let her into my sacred spaces of not knowing. This is not easy, but it's good.

I am also the parent of two adolescents. Talk about spaces of not knowing! How do I best protect them? When must I not protect them? How can I honor their sensibilities yet find a way to hold them close? Should I draw a line in the sand or take them to the beach? In some real ways, every now and then, my uncle's spirit and his poem allow me to host these moments of adolescent parenting with less frustration and anxiety and more intrigue and joy.

> *I read my uncle's poem and come to trust that this era of my life can be trusted, can be grace-filled, can bring me to unexpected arrivals.*

I am forty-seven—mid-life and then some. There is a reason that the words *mid-life* and *crisis* are usually in the same phrase. Mid-life is the precursor of the diminishment of *late-life*. In lieu of the red sports car, which because of my financial limits I can't afford, I read my uncle's poem and come to trust that this era of my life can be trusted, can be grace-filled, can bring me to unexpected arrivals.

I recently visited my uncle in his nursing home outside of Milwaukee. He emerged out of the elevator on his scooter, having more or less given up on the walking enterprise. By way of greeting he says, "You know what the problem is with this shiny new scooter, Terry?" I play into his hand. "No, Uncle Bob, what is the problem with your shiny new scooter?" He responds, "It's a chick magnet!" He raises his arms as wide as he is able and laughs as long as he ever did. I walk into his arms and join in the laughter. We linger in the embrace, then our laughter subsides. He points his chick magnet in the direction of what he calls the "really sick" wing of the home and says, "Come with me, Terry. I'll show you where I'm finding life these days."

I follow him. He is my hero.

A Table for One

by Helen Reichert Lambin

hen my husband, Henry, died on January 20, 1996, time became a prison for me. My best friend of more than thirty years was dead. But I knew that statistically I could live another thirty years (just as my mother had after the death of my dad). Thirty years! It was hard enough getting through twenty-four hours.

I am lucky to have three grown children, one of them with children of his own. I am fortunate to have some good friends. I have other blessings as well. But that wasn't enough. I was here. Henry wasn't. How was I going to survive all those years without him?

Eventually I did what prisoners have done from time immemorial. I divided the approximate time I had left into what seemed to be more manageable blocks—360 of them, to be exact. Three hundred sixty was in some ways an absurd number for the purpose of dividing something. But at least it was something I could measure and did make some sense: If I lived the expected thirty years more, I would live another 360 months—the same number of months I had lived with

Henry. I might not be able to face thirty years alone, but even I had to agree that I could survive 1/360th of it.

—

The first couple of years were simply a matter of survival—day by day, month by month. I became an expert on fractions. Two months: 1/180th; three months: 1/120th; four months: 1/90th; six months: 1/60th; nine months: 1/40th; two years: 1/15th.

I still didn't think in terms of plans, changes or goals in my life. I was just making the hash marks on the wall. The only thing I looked forward to was the earliest date at which I could take my retirement.

I began to write about my grief: the thoughts, feelings, pain, loneliness, anger and hopes that everyone who has lost a loved one experiences.

After the first few blocks of time, I began to write about my grief: the thoughts, feelings, pain, loneliness, anger and hopes that everyone who has lost a loved one experiences. I wasn't writing for any particular purpose, but I found myself writing to and for people just like me—women I didn't know but with whom I felt a peculiar kinship. I wrote about how it felt to be a widow, something about which I had no particular expertise other than being one. My writing continued for almost a year and a half, and suddenly I found that I had survived 18 of the 360 blocks I had left.

I was still standing. Although that seemed achievement enough, I was beginning to visualize the rest of my life. It was a grid—six squares across, five down, with one square filled in for each year that I survived. But I suspected that maybe there should be more to my life than filling in annual squares.

In the middle of the second year after Henry's death, two significant things happened. In June I completed the manuscript of a book, titled simply *The Death of a Husband,* and turned it in to my publisher. Writing it had given some sense of structure and purpose to my life, something to fill each 1/360th section of my life, but suddenly the book was completed. It wasn't that I stopped thinking of Henry at that point. (I still think of him many times every day.) It was a matter of trying to think of what was I going to do *now* with the rest of my life.

Then in October I took the long awaited early retirement. I was liberated from my private basement office—composed of two cheerless rooms with glass block and smoked glass windows. Through them only shadows of the outside world could penetrate. Working in this environment had only helped reinforce my image of myself as a prisoner of time.

You might say that my wanting to have more time for myself when I was already trying to count off what I had left may seem illogical, but grief is seldom logical. Here is how I thought: *Now I can at least use more of those 1/360th segments as I choose, rather than as someone else chooses for me.* Henry would have appreciated the not-so-subtle difference.

Now that I had more time to decide what I wanted to do, I found I had a much more difficult decision to make: Who was I going to *be*?

I had never had a problem with identity before. I was *me*. I might not have been completely satisfied with the *me I was*, but I always knew who that was. But no longer. I knew who I *had been*, but now I no longer felt like that person. I didn't feel like anyone else either, but I certainly didn't feel like *me*.

As a possible part of my identity, the eccentric traveler seemed a stretch.

One positive image of a woman alone came to me from books. This was the eccentric older woman, often English (think of characters played by Maggie Smith, Judy Dench, Vanessa Redgrave, that sort of thing), who traveled on her own—respectably, economically and confidently. She could flit off to Europe or Egypt, find her way around a strange city, and request a table for one without so much as turning a single gray hair.

But as a possible part of *my* identity, the eccentric traveler seemed a stretch. I did not yet even admit to being an "older" woman, much less consider myself eccentric. I certainly no longer felt independent. And I wasn't even English. Still, without being aware of it, in 1998, some two years (or 24/360ths) after being widowed, I began to try to break out of the jail of my widowhood.

It was a very gradual approach. For one thing, there was economic reality. Frequent foreign travel was not an option. For another, I had to prepare myself to jump off this particular cliff. I had felt much more independent when I was with Henry than I did without him. Finally, I had to learn at least enough of a foreign language to travel alone.

My first test was to go for nine days to London, where my younger daughter met me for several days. I was only on my own for part of the time, and Londoners spoke my native language (more or less). But it was a start.

The next spring I joined a tour of Spain that offered participants some significant free time on their own, and I added three solo days in Madrid.

In the third year after Henry's death (after I had clocked 1/10 of my allotted life-after-his-death time), I stayed in a convenient and reasonable Left Bank hotel in Paris and lined up all my own local tours. I had finally done it: on my own and eccentric as hell!

But on each trip I brooded all the way over. How different it would be if Henry were with me. What was I thinking of? What was I doing and why was I doing it? What if I got lost? What if I couldn't even find my way around well enough to get lost? I generally decided that once I got wherever I was going I would do the best I could, but I determined that I would not enjoy it. And I promised myself that once I got home I would never do anything like this again!

Yet each time, once I arrived it somehow felt all right. I learned about buying transit passes to simplify travel by subway or bus, and how to read city and metro maps. I learned that when I did get myself lost I could find my way back again. And on each trip there were times when I wished with unshed tears that Henry could see the wonders of what I was seeing.

—

I next broke my independent travel pattern for an organized tour of majestic Newfoundland and Labrador. Everything was well taken care of, but I returned feeling deprived. I missed the challenges and rewards of traveling on my own, such as blending into the scenery in ways that are impossible in a group.

I made up for that lack of challenge in the seventh year. (I was now almost 1/4th of the way through my projected widowhood.) Two years before I had seen on exhibit some Venetian paintings by artist Thomas Parrish. I knew immediately that I had to see, at least once in my lifetime, the paths of lamplight on the waters of the Grand Canal. Venice, city of canals, however, marked a kind of watershed. For me, just getting there offered more challenge than I actually needed.

In the first place, this was the spring of 2002, the spring immediately following the tragedy of September 11. Like everything else in life, travel had changed. But I didn't realize how much so until I tried to get to Venice.

In addition, going to Venice was a more complicated business than traveling to other places. There were no direct flights, so I would have to change planes in Germany or Italy. (Changing planes by oneself in a foreign country is a different experience than doing so with someone else to share the confusion.)

Furthermore, and for me far more intimidating, was the question of how to get from airport to hotel. The airport was apparently on the far side of a really large lagoon. Unlike other cities, you couldn't just take an airport shuttle bus or hire a taxi to deliver you to the hotel door. There are no cars of any kind in Venice proper, because there are no streets on which to drive. There are only walkways, bridges and canals, and for transportation there are only boats—big boats, little boats, public boats, private boats, police boats, fireboats, water taxis and, of course, gondolas. Even a water taxi can take you only as far as the nearest landing stage in Venice. After that, you and your luggage are on your own.

Various guidebooks noted that Venice is legendarily easy to get lost in. This was supposed to be part of its charm.

Finally, various guidebooks noted that Venice is legendarily easy to get lost in. This was supposed to be part of its charm. (Miss Marple to the rescue! or Oh, Henry!)

But if I didn't go to Venice right then I was afraid I might lose my nerve—not only to see Venice but to continue my jailbreak. It had been more than two years since I'd traveled independently. I was 24/360ths older. So, with trepidation I made reservations for a five-day Venice stay.

—

For simplicity's sake, I chose a good hotel in the working class area of Venice, which is less costly and crowded than the tourist areas. Since it was on the Grand Canal, I figured I should be able to find it. (A "Grand Canal" sounded hard to miss.) On the way over the Atlantic I tried to repress visions of my trundling a rolling suitcase endlessly through the back streets of Venice in search of the ever-elusive hotel. But this time I didn't even ask myself why I was doing all this. I had remembered well the words of my husband, a psychologist with the Veterans Administration: "As you grow older you have to be careful about what you stop doing. Otherwise you may find you don't start doing it again."

> I had remembered well the words of my husband: "As you grow older you have to be careful about what you stop doing. Otherwise you may find you don't start doing it again."

Much to my surprise, I did find my way to the hotel, via two public water buses, which saved me the cost of a taxi and seemed the sort of thing any eccentric and economic traveler would do. En route I made the acquaintance of a group of Italian schoolgirls on a field trip with their teacher. On hearing my Italian phrases they guessed that I was German, Spanish, or yes, *English*. This was a personal triumph that I thoroughly savored. The unexpected in Venice *was* part of the charm.

I had promised myself paths of lamplight rippling on the Grand Canal. So on one quiet weeknight, I made a reservation in the hotel dining room for a table at a canal-side window. It was, of course, a table for one.

Once, not too many 360ths before, I would have felt terribly self-conscious. A table-for-one dinner is radically different from lunching alone. But now, for the moment at least, I was that eccentric, *slightly* older woman who could travel independently with ease and grace. And I had even been taken for an Englishwoman!

Over mellow Italian wine and savored Italian seafood, I watched the blue-gray Venetian twilight turn to darkness. When the waiter appeared with the check, he said gently, first in Italian, then in English: "Do not be in a hurry to pay this. Take time to enjoy what you see."

The canal-side lamps were lit, mingling with the moonlight, sending rippling paths of silver-gold on the black waters of the Canal. How I wished that Henry could see what I was seeing. And I wondered if, in some mystical but real way, he could.

Would it have been better if Henry were there with me, at a table for *two*? There is no doubt. It would have been perfect. I know because we shared a number of perfect moments in our married life. But still, this time alone was perfect in its own way. It was a time of enchantment, a gift of time, a gift I know Henry would have wanted me to enjoy. I am grateful for it.

—

One of the things Henry's death has taught me is that new life can arise—*in spite of* and *out of* the pain of loss. These blessings do not necessarily follow our plans or rules. I had to learn to let go of—or go around—all the "if only's."

It is not that I have "gotten over" losing Henry. I cannot do that. I will always miss him. There are losses that can prove to be blessings in disguise, but I do not believe the death of a beloved spouse is ever one of them. A world with Henry was a much better one than one without him.

There have been and continue to be blessings that have manifested themselves in a variety of ways and have transformed my sorrow into something holy, tender and somehow transcendent.

But there have been and continue to be blessings that have manifested themselves in a variety of ways and have transformed my sorrow into something holy, tender and somehow transcendent.

I still see the joys and passions Henry shared with our children: his love of music in our son, his vision in the photographs taken by our older daughter, his deep respect for the past in the preservation work (and sometime pack-rat activity) of our younger daughter. This is surely a blessing.

Other widows have told me that *The Death of A Husband* had meaning for them because it told *their* stories and articulated *their* experiences. Henry was by profession and personality a nurturer. In his work at the Veterans Hospital he was committed to offering whatever healing he could. It seems fitting that through his death, as well as his life, some healing could be provided others. This is another blessing.

Learning to travel independently, to become to some extent that eccentric, older woman I always admired is a blessing. It has given me the opportunity to experience wonderful moments and anticipate other such moments. It has restored in me a feeling of confidence. But it has also done much more for me than that, although I have come to realize it only recently. For me, my travel is a *symbol*, a symbol of being *part* of the story instead of merely looking on.

Because what I have learned from Henry's death is that not only are there blessings in less-than-perfect moments but that sorrow and loss lead beyond themselves and beyond time.

So I almost had it right when I began counting by 1/360ths after Henry's death. Almost. For I have since learned that time, which had seemed a prison to be endured, had become both a gift and a responsibility to be used as well as is humanly possible. I learned that there is much more to grieving than simply filling all those blank squares. It is what you fill them with.

Unbounded Beneficence

by Kass Dotterweich

I t might be an unwanted pregnancy, Kass, but it's not an unwanted child." As I sat in the chilly, dark church that late autumn evening, the memory of my friend's words seared my soul. Everything in me wanted that trite euphemism to be a truth about the reality of my life in that moment, but it was not. I simply could not separate the *pregnancy* from the *child*. It *was* an unwanted pregnancy, and so it *was*....

Even now, over twenty years later, I cannot finish that thought.

It was the fall of 1982. I was the mother of five children, the youngest barely a year old. I was unemployed, and the national manufacturing firm my husband worked for was on strike (making our household income a full $45.00 a week— the strike stipend he made for walking the picket lines). We had received notice from the bank threatening foreclosure on our house if we didn't negotiate a plan for our back mortgage payments, and all the utilities were in arrears.

After spending hours on the phone that day trying to

explain our situation to these respective entities, I was deeply dispirited, embarrassed, frightened—and angry.

—

My anger always frightens me. After all, anger is not an acceptable emotion, so much so that it ranks right up there with the seven deadly ("capital") sins. "A fool gives full vent to anger, but the wise quietly holds it back" (Proverbs 29:11). "Do not let the sun go down on your anger" (Ephesians 4:26). And surely one's anger with God must be the ultimate sin, that blasphemous behavior that can never be forgiven: "Whoever blasphemes against the Holy Spirit can never have forgiveness, but is guilty of an eternal sin" (Mark 3:29).

As I sat in church attending our parish reconciliation service that night over twenty years ago, I was an angry woman—angry with God.

And then there was the lived reality of the consequences of anger that I had learned only too well as a child. Expressions of anger brought only painful results: ostracism ("Go to your room"); humiliation ("You should be ashamed of yourself"); or returned anger ("Don't you dare").

Yet as I sat in church attending our parish reconciliation service that night over twenty years ago, I was an angry woman—angry with God. The venom of my thoughts—

hardly registering as prayer—went something like this: "Sure, God. You say, 'My ways are not your ways.' That empty platitude means nothing in the realm of reality. The bank doesn't care about *your way*, God! I cannot sit down and write out a check to the gas company in the amount of *your way. Your way* is not going to feed these children!"

Driving my anger was the fact that I was a *good Catholic*. In those days, that meant first and foremost that my husband and I were using the natural family planning method of birth control. According to the literature and training classes we had attended, the success rate of that method was so high that my becoming pregnant most likely meant that *I* was the one who had messed up!

So in the incense-filled shadows of church that night, I both seethed with the deadly sin of anger and bore the shame of failure.

———

I was in that pew for only one reason: so that my two oldest children would "go to confession." That is what we Catholic parents did on Saturdays back then, and I was in no mood to rock that particular boat. I was not, however, the least bit open to even the remotest possibility that God's grace could penetrate the fortress of my anger and resentment. In fact, the rage was so consuming that I couldn't even "want to want" to pray, as Thomas Merton described the minimal pre-prayer state.

I cared nothing about seeking God's forgiveness in the midst of my despair, and I certainly had nothing of a sacramental nature to celebrate. I was lost in the stranglehold of anger, indignation and self-righteousness; my emotions defined my existence. It's not that my anger drove me to deny God's existence. After all, I had to cling to God so that I would have someone to blame. Rather, I denied God's power and presence. I accused God of favoritism, meanness and negligence—not of non-existence.

> *As my children knelt for their prayers of penance, I suddenly rose and headed for the confessional.*

Although my body throbbed with the heartbeat of new life, I felt nothing but faithless, spiritless, spiteful, deadly anger. I had no *"Let it be done unto me"* to offer to myself, to my family, to my God...or to my unborn child.

As my children knelt for their prayers of penance—probably the *pro-forma* three Our Fathers and three Hail Marys that most kids' confessions in those days received and deserved—I suddenly rose and headed for the confessional.

What did I think I was doing? I had no intention of celebrating the sacrament. I was in no mood for reconciliation with anyone, least of all a representative of the God who had gotten me into this predicament. Yet for some reason, pulled by some primordial urge, I stepped into the dimly lit room and pulled the door closed behind me. Only in reflecting at length on that moment over the years have I come to realize what motivated me—at least on the surface—that holy night so long ago. It was exhaustion, a desire to avoid conflict and unpleasantry at all cost. I knew that I did not have the energy to squirm and stammer excuses—thus adding guilt to my anger—when my children launched into their inevitable interrogation in the car on the way home: "Why didn't you go to confession, Mom?"

Now, is that a stupid reason to go to confession, or what?

—

Although the priest's smile was welcoming and peaceful, I remained rigid and remorseless as I slipped into the rote ritual so familiar yet so pointless: "Bless me, Father, for I have sinned."

Then silence—a deep, heavy, engulfing silence—descended like a pall. I found I couldn't continue. Yet as I struggled to maintain my composure, tears surfaced and rolled down my cheeks.

"What is it, Kass?" the priest asked as he handed me a box of tissues.

And then, the deluge. For the next twenty minutes, amidst wracking sobs and constant nose blowing, I poured out my soul's desolate and barren reality. I didn't care about the niceties of sacramental form; I didn't worry whether or not I had the components of true contrition; I wasn't even sorry for anything that I had done (other than get pregnant, which was *not* my fault).

But the priest's simple question—"What is it, Kass?"—had sliced through my defenses like a scalpel lancing a boil, and the reality of my own human weakness—indeed, the weakness of the human condition itself—entered my awareness.

It wasn't as if I consciously and purposefully gave in to God's will. That would have been too easy—and too shallow. Rather, in a way that I still cannot explain, the pure and unconditional love of God somehow entered that small shadowy room and pierced my angry heart so that grace could become incarnate in the child within my womb.

Here's what happened. I mumbled the usual act of contrition—I guess—and the priest must have offered absolution, for that same deep, heavy and engulfing silence had returned. I was aware that my breathing was shallow but peaceful, and that I felt a sense of being saturated with something beyond myself.

"For your penance, Kass," the priest said as he rose and knelt down next to my chair, "you and I will sing together 'Joy to the World.'" And without waiting for me to respond—probably knowing I would object—Father started, coaxing me all the way: "'*Joy to the world,*' come on, Kass…'*the Lord has come.*' Sing, Kass! '*Let earth receive her King.*'

Sing, Kass. Sing right now. This is your part! Sing!"

With a mixture of absolute embarrassment and total confusion, I whined the next line of lyrics along with that dear man: *"Let every heart, prepare him room."'*

With those words, the image of my unborn child flooded my mind, and I heard my soul's unique song of prayer: "Let *my own* heart prepare him room." In that moment, I not only gave birth to a lasting and passionate love for my sixth child, but I came face to face with the ultimate and gentle power of God. There, in that place where I did not want to be, I realized that the presence of God and the grace of the Spirit were far more powerful than my anger and pride.

> *I realized that the presence of God and the grace of the Spirit were far more powerful than my anger and pride.*

When I emerged from the confessional, someone had already dimmed the lights in the church, the candles had been extinguished, and my children had evidently wandered outdoors to await their very sinful mother. After all, I'd been in the confessional a rather unusually long length of time—one usually reserved for the greatest of sinners.

That sixth child? Howard Thomas Dotterweich was born on July 19, 1983, bringing to our family the joys, satisfactions and challenges unique to every newborn. Today, he is an Eagle Scout, a Twenty-First-Century Scholar, and a member of the National Honor Society. As he pursues his college education, he is participating in a program to help him decide if he is being called to join the Dominican order of priests.

The strike? It ended, but then it turned into an extended layoff that continued until Howard was two months old. We managed to survive with financial assistance from family, friends, government programs and our parish St. Vincent de Paul Society.

And the anger? Over the years, the vicissitudes of life—dishonesty and betrayal in relationships, the sudden death of my father, the loss of a job, the miscarriage of a grandchild—have given rise many times to the savage onslaught of anger in my breast. Many times I've heard that desperate voice of helplessness calling me once again into the darkness of rage—and many times I've succumbed to that call.

But never again has the anger driven me to deny the power of God's hidden presence. Never again have I entertained my own prideful, self-serving and self-righteous anger to the point of feeling beyond God's love and grace. And this has been the true blessing, the unbounded beneficence, of my unplanned, unwanted and unforgettable pregnancy.

Depressed?
Who, Me?

by Patrick Hannon

If I should pass the tomb of Jonah
I would stop there and sit for awhile;
Because I was swallowed one time deep in the dark
And came out alive after all.

        —Carl Sandburg

The first thing you need to know about me is that I never wanted to move to the Midwest.

Seven weeks into my first year at Notre Dame High School in Niles, a suburb just outside of Chicago, I'm sitting at a table on an unusually cold October evening talking with the mother of one of my students, and she is asking me where I came from. When I tell her California, she looks at me quizzically—you know, with the horrified gawk usually reserved for sideshow exhibits in traveling carnivals. "Why in God's name would you want to move from California to Chicago?" she asks in all sincerity.

Why, indeed? But I tell her what I want to believe: I love a new challenge; I heard Chicago is a great town; I wanted to get back into teaching.

I go on and on, but the honest-to-God truth is that it was the vow of obedience—the quiet sibling of those sacred vows members of religious communities make—that got me here. It was obedience, and obedience alone. As I said, the first thing you need to know about me for the purpose of this story is that I never wanted to move to the Midwest.

—

My students—all male—think celibacy must be the toughest vow to embrace, and given their hormonal state, I don't blame them. Or sometimes they figure it must be the vow of poverty, given their own lifestyles and aspirations. ("How do you *live* on only three hundred bucks a month, Father?") But I promise you that it is really and truly the vow of obedience that has kept me up nights, sweating and rethinking the trajectory of my life and making me more humble than I ever wanted to be.

> It is really and truly the vow of obedience that has kept me up nights.

I suspect I am not unlike most everyone else in this regard, especially spouses and parents. Stitched into married life is a kind of obedience that requires great sacrifice too. Both theologically and practically speaking, obedience means our lives are never truly our own. Parents and spouses live that truth out every day, and so do men and women who take religious vows.

So it happened that five years ago I packed all of my belongings into cardboard boxes and made the trek from San Francisco to Chicago. I was beginning a new ministry in a new town with a group of Holy Cross priests I did not know. I was thirty-nine years old—a novice middle-ager living two thousand miles away from my nearest kin. I told my family and friends that this would be a three-year gig and that with my provincial superior's blessing, and God willing, I would return, like the prodigal son, to bask once again in the warmth of familial love and west coast sun.

—

The second thing you need to know about me is that I'm Irish. There is a strain of us called the "I'm-never-truly-happy-unless-I'm-sad" Irish. Depression runs in my family, and all of my brothers and sisters and I agree it is because of the Celtic blood that courses through our veins. The Irish writer Edna O'Brien put it this way: "When anyone asks me about the Irish character, I say look at the trees. Maimed, stark and misshapen, but ferociously tenacious." We're the kind of Irishmen who are genuinely cheerful on the outside. We exhibit a spirit that betrays a gritty determination to endure, but on the inside, well, there sits the sad poet.

Now, our *particular* strand of Irish, namely, the Hannon clan, finds its greatest joy in pleasing others. Growing up, we were the ones you wanted to invite to your parties or enlist for some huge project. We were the best lab partners in chemistry class. We lived to make other people happy. The greatest sin any of us could commit was the sin of disappointing someone else. (Though we only occasionally practiced such generosity among our siblings, the rest of the world loved us Hannon kids.)

—

These two dominant traits—the propensity toward melancholy and the desire to please—finally came home to roost for me seven weeks into my stint at Notre Dame High School.

I had moved because I was asked to, because I wanted to believe that I was a team player, because I wanted to be an obedient son (read: please my superiors). But, unbeknownst to almost everyone at the school—my colleagues, students, and most of my Holy Cross confreres—I was being sucked deeper and deeper into an unfamiliar darkness, a darkness I began to fear would swallow me whole.

My depression was like waking up on a different planet. I distinctly remember walking one morning in early August along the breezeway that connects the school with the priests' residence. It was the first day of classes, and I had a growing feeling of apprehension and uncertainty that I had never before experienced. At first, I dismissed it as first day jitters. After all, it had been nine years since I had taught full time. If I hadn't been nervous, I would have been worried! (How's that for Irish optimism?)

But somehow I knew that this was more than nervousness. Much the way one senses with the first scratch in the throat that it's more than a cold, I knew that I was dealing with something far more serious than stage fright. Yet the farthest point on my new horizon bore only the faintest hint of the brewing storm.

It was the beginning of my first—but not my last—episode of major depression.

I walked into my first period class, British Literature with seniors, completely out of my element. I was standing before what appeared to be the entire offensive and defensive lines of the varsity football team, twenty-eight young men who carried themselves with a Chicago swagger and spoke with a kind of street-smart cockiness that had me pining immediately for those kind old ladies that kept me knee-deep in devotion and chocolate-chip cookies at the parish I had left behind.

I made it through that first day—barely—and collapsed in a chair in my bedroom that afternoon. I slept through dinner. It was the beginning of my first—but not my last—episode of major depression.

My students were (and are) amazing human beings. After a few short weeks I got used to the all-male environment of Notre Dame. In many respects it is like a tight-knit family, a fraternity of brothers. It amazes me still to witness the kind of fierce loyalty and pride such a learning environment engenders in the hearts of young men. In my first weeks in the teaching saddle, the Dons of Notre Dame (a Don is a Gentleman) coaxed the best out of me.

Beowulf, Blake, Shakespeare, Shelly: I was determined to shape their minds and hearts with the tools of prose and verse. Knowing how much I loved literature and writing, they mostly went along, feigning disinterest but secretly hoping I would inspire them.

It took every ounce of energy to get out of bed.

But even as I summoned my will and energy every morning to teach, I was beginning to die a little every day. The seeping sadness took over my sleep first. I began waking up in the middle of the night and lay there until together my alarm clock and I welcomed the dawn. It took every ounce of energy to get out of bed. I would sit through Morning Prayer with my Holy Cross community, and I found many of the psalms bemusing at best, cruelly ironic at worst. "Save me, God," Psalm 69 begins, "for the waters have reached my neck. I have sunk into the mire of the deep where there is no foothold. I am weary for crying out." And Psalm 63: "O God, you are my God—for you I long. For you my soul is thirsting; my body pines for you like a dry, weary land without water."

Only later would I come to appreciate that the gnawing pain of anguish that I felt those mornings was prayer, and though it seemed as if God had turned a deaf ear to my constant pleas, in retrospect, God was there with me, sharing my suffering, making it His own.

—

By the time I arrived in my classroom each morning, I was usually fine. I thoroughly enjoyed the respite that my work-load provided me: teaching, counseling, moderating a club. I actually did a phenomenal job hiding the truth; and I'm glad I did. My students needed me to be their teacher, and they needed me to be at my best. Whatever personal trials I was enduring were kept secret.

I recall later that semester one of my seniors asking me with a well-honed skepticism how it was possible for me to be so happy and positive all the time. Not telling him the truth—that even getting dressed was a decision I made each day and that the decision caused me great pain—brought me secret satisfaction as well. Inside, I was like the poet's Irish tree: "maimed, stark, misshapen." But outside I was still able to be "ferociously tenacious."

My depression really came down to a lack of trust. I was having a very difficult time accepting the possibility that it was God's will for me to be in Illinois, teaching English to a bunch of boys I didn't know. It made absolutely no sense that I should be exiled so far away from family and friends, from anything that was familiar to me. I was deeply lonely, and that loneliness drew me into a defensive, isolating crouch. I spent a lot of time by myself.

Weekends were the worst, for the one thing that kept me tethered to any semblance of stability was my academic routine. Many a weekend night I spent on the phone with a few trusted friends, and then finally my brothers and sisters, crying my eyes out. It wasn't supposed to be this hard! I had already buried my mother and father and the one grandparent I had ever known. I knew what it was like to love and lose. And though I had long accepted the fact that life could be cruel and bitter at times, it seemed ludicrous to have to walk that lonely road severed from my loved ones, all because I had made a promise to obey my religious superiors.

Folks often ask me how we are to discern God's will for us. I tell them that we must always discern first what *our* heart's deepest desire is, and having done that, we will discover what *God's* deepest desire is for us as well.

At first I thought my deepest desire was to return home and go to as many Oakland Athletic games as possible. I thought my heart's deepest desire was to take a bottle of California wine to Baker Beach at dusk and toast the sunset as it slipped behind the placid Pacific, casting the Golden Gate Bridge in a light both hieratic and profound. I thought my heart's deepest desire was to "get the hell out of Dodge." Every night I prayed to God to instruct me in His ways, to help me make sense of my suffering. Every morning I prayed—actually demanded—that God let me know, in a timely manner, what I was supposed to do. And every night and every morning the only words I heard from God in my heart were two: "Trust me." And those two words depressed me to the bottom of my soul.

I began to lose weight. When I went home for a quick visit over Thanksgiving weekend, my family thought I had cancer. I finally began to let my brothers in community know that I was in a desperate struggle to survive. Such is the insidious evil of depression that it makes us believe things that simply aren't true. I thought I was a complete flop in and out of the classroom. I looked at myself in the mirror and observed a failure—a weak, frightened, pathetic creature—despite every assurance by others to the contrary. I simply did not believe them.

"Trust me," was all God would say to me in those dark days.

Nonetheless, I held on. I had too much in the game now to fold. I was going to see this hand through. "Trust me," was all God would say to me in those dark days. It was a gamble; but I hadn't much else left to lose.

━

That December, right near the end of the first semester, I met with a mother of one of my seniors. She had asked to see me because she was concerned about her son's academic performance. The boy was not a particularly disciplined student, and he was struggling to maintain a D in my course. I assumed he wasn't faring much better in his other classes.

The mother was not much older than I. She was a single mom, working two jobs so that her son might attend

Catholic high school. At one point in our conversation, after assuring her that I would continue to work with her son so that he would get a passing grade, I began to tell her of the potential I saw in his writing. Sure, he was a bit sloppy and inconsistent in his prose, I said, but he had a bit of the poet in him. I showed her some of his writing and pointed out where I saw real promise. With enough hard work and encouragement, I told her, I thought he could be a promising writer.

I realized that she was hearing—maybe for the first time in a long, long time—that she was not a failure.

And then I thanked her. I told her that poets are almost always born first in the hearts of their mothers and that it is usually the case that writers are nurtured by the encouragement of the ones who love them. In her son's case, it was she who needed to be thanked for tending to a young mind and heart in its most formative period. I thanked her for being a great mom.

Suddenly, she began to cry. I knew immediately that they were tears of both joy and sadness.

I realized that she was hearing—maybe for the first time in a long, long time—that she was not a failure, that she really was doing an amazing job raising a son all on her own. I saw sadness because maybe she had come perilously close to surrendering to the darkness of despair.

"Father Pat," she told me, "there's something you need to know, something none of John's classmates know. Tomorrow," she continued, "John will be celebrating his first year of sobriety. He is a recovering heroin addict."

She proceeded to tell me of her son's middle-school years when he had first experimented with marijuana and then alcohol, and then how in the eighth grade he had gotten hooked on heroin. She told me of his slow progress back to health and how grateful he was to be at Notre Dame because it placed a healthy distance between him and those with whom he associated during his drinking and drugging days. She told me how he was so looking forward to the next day, when he would celebrate his "first birthday" off drugs.

By the end of our conversation we both were in tears, and afterward it began to dawn on me that maybe God had indeed answered my prayers. Perhaps I now knew why I had been asked to move to Chicago. Perhaps it was my heart's deepest desire to stay. In one brief encounter with the mother of one of my students, both of our suffering had been laid bare, and for both of us the suffering had become redemptive.

Thomas Merton often talked about the idea of redemptive suffering. For Christians, suffering of any sort becomes redemptive when we willingly hand it over to God, trusting in the healing power of the redeeming cross of His Son, Jesus Christ.

John's mother and I had walked alone for a long time up our separate Calvary hills until—at that one graced moment in time—we began to walk together.

Those first months at Notre Dame were for me three long days in the tomb. I was asked by my superiors to come to Chicago—unbeknownst to them or to me—so that I might come to trust God more completely. I had to leave home and loved ones in order to see my familial and tribal predisposition for melancholy as a gift of sorts and not a burden.

At the end of Mark's gospel, when the three women arrive at the tomb of Jesus only to find that the huge stone covering the entrance had been rolled away, they saw a young man sitting on the right side, clothed in a white robe. "Do not be afraid," the young man urged them. "You seek Jesus of Nazareth, the crucified. He has been raised; he is not here!"

Five years ago, I was swallowed by a deep darkness; and for a while I lay helpless in a tomb. And then one day, a young man, one who had spent the better part of a year putting on new garments of sobriety, garments that would heal the syringe marks on his body and make him new again, rolled the stone away for me. His name was John, and he was the angel who came to tell me that there was reason to trust, to hope, to hold on.

The Heart Speaks

Robert Raccuglia

At age forty-three, I experienced the heart attack as a sudden intrusion into my life. I guess they call it a heart *attack* for a reason. Mine came on a little subtler than the sharp spear in the chest that some people get, but I sure didn't see it coming. Being relatively fit, a vegetarian no less, I had no obvious warning signs.

The first surprising little twinges began on a cold December Monday while I was walking to work. They continued from time to time for the next several days. By Friday, sharp pains in my chest accompanied any little exertion. So I finally called the doctor. At least at this point, I figured, I would only lose an afternoon of work to get it checked out.

If you think I was a little slow on the uptake, it gets worse. When the doctor told me to come right in, I agreed. But I told him that first I was going to stop at my daughter's school to see her in the class Christmas pageant. (I underplayed to him the frequency and severity of the chest pains.) As I descended into the subway station, the pain felt even more serious than before. An hour later, however, I was at

Roosevelt School edging my way into a crowded classroom of excited parents. As I settled into a tiny chair in the back corner, the extent of my foolishness began to sink in, but not yet fully.

By the time the Holy Family found its humble lodgings, the discomfort in my chest was demanding all of my attention. Sure, I wanted to see Clare in her white robes, wings and aluminum foil halo, but I now realized that a straight path to the hospital, several days overdue, would have been a wiser course. I considered leaving before the Magi arrived with their gifts, but I would have had to step over a dozen enraptured parents, distracting and annoying them, and perhaps embarrassing my daughter. (What would be worse for her, I wondered, to have her father disrupt the pageant with an awkward, premature departure or to have him slump down in cardiac failure along the back bulletin board? I decided to risk the latter possibility, figuring that it would be quieter and perhaps go unnoticed until after the final scene.)

> *Sometimes life lets us get away with utter stupidity.*

Sometimes life lets us get away with utter stupidity. I got to see my daughter in angelic garb herald the birth of the Christ child without my dying in the process. And finally, barely, I made it to the medical center. After a few tests, the doctor introduced me to a strange new world in which I traded in my civilian clothes for a white gown and where the concerns of work and Christmas preparations faded to the background.

It seemed surreal to find myself admitted to a hospital for the first time in my life. On the night before my surgery, the old man in the next bed wept in fear of the bypass that was scheduled for him in the morning. I was expecting "just" an angioplasty for myself and felt badly for my roommate, but I congratulated myself on how calmly I was handling my situation. It must be due to my deeply spiritual nature, I figured. When things went badly for me the next day during the procedure and the doctor informed me that I needed emergency bypass surgery as soon as the surgeon could be called in, I took the news with what seemed to me courageous peacefulness and acceptance, joking with my family out in the hallway to reassure them as we waited for the surgical team to assemble. Only later did I learn that my brave spirit of equanimity was mainly due to the massive dose of valium that had been given me for the angioplasty. The tranquilizing drug, combined with some self-delusional mental trick that had me half thinking that all this was happening to someone else, kept me unreasonably relaxed. It *still* hadn't totally registered that I was the one going under the knife.

Only when I awoke from the quadruple bypass operation did the seriousness of my situation really grab my full attention. The ventilator, drainage tubes, IVs and the pain from the foot-long incision bisecting my chest made it hard to ignore. Heart surgery may be a routine procedure for the surgeons, but it is something quite out of the ordinary for the patient. I had no choice but to take notice of what had happened to me and to wonder what it was telling me.

As blithely as I had treated the onset of the heart attack, the doctor informed me that I easily could have died. I was fortunate to be alive. I would need to take care of my heart in a conscious way from this time forward. Until then, I had taken good health as a given. I took pride in it, as if I had done something to deserve it. Ironically, my return to health came not through my merit but in spite of the foolish way that I delayed getting treatment. My health was an undeserved gift, one to be appreciated and nourished.

The heart attack was a gift of sorts on another level. If part of becoming a mature person is facing reality and acting upon it, the health crisis may have been for me a strange, if unwanted, blessing. It was as if my life were saying to me: "Now that I have your attention, let's have a look at the way that you face up to things." I was George Bailey of *It's a Wonderful Life* being rescued from the brink with a chance to start over.

Lying in bed, I recalled a quote of Elizabeth Kübler-Ross: "You will not grow if you sit in a beautiful flower garden, but you will grow if you are sick, if you are in pain, if you experience losses, and if you do not put your head in the sand. Take pain as a gift to you with a very, very specific purpose."

If you do not put your head in the sand. Isn't that what I had done in ignoring the warning signs about the heart attack? Wasn't that the strategy that I had used (unsuccessfully) with many difficulties in my life? Maybe now I was being given a chance to do things differently.

I came out of the surgery wanting to be a new man. Being a religiously inclined person, I envisioned dramatic changes in my life. I imagined myself not just as George Bailey but as Saul getting knocked from his horse on the road to Damascus or Ignatius of Loyola, who was transformed by reading the Lives of the Saints during a long convalescence from a battle injury. Could my recuperation period lead to a similar reassessment and redirecting of my life? A friend had even suggested that I look at the weeks of sedentary rehab as a thirty-day retreat.

Looking back from the perspective of seven years, I see the heart attack as a subtly transforming event in my life.

The Big Conversion did not happen in my case, however. I wish I could say that I changed dramatically. I wish that I could say that I gained enlightenment. The truth is that there was no unmistakable overnight conversion. But looking back from the perspective of seven years, I see the heart attack as a subtly transforming event in my life. It made me face some aspects of my life (and death) a little more squarely.

The French novelist Leon Bloy said, "There are places in the heart which do not yet exist, and into them enters suffering that they may have existence." An experience that I had a few nights after my surgery while listening to the radio as I lay awake in the middle of the night seemed to hint at that reality. There was a report of the uncovering of a mass grave of several thousand Muslims and Croats in a mine in Bosnia. Busloads of victims had been taken to the mine to be systematically shot day after day for weeks. I don't know how many horrific stories I have heard or read over the years from places like Vietnam, Rwanda, Chechnya, Iraq or even the west side of Chicago. Always they are shocking, but on this night I felt an unusual personal sorrow for the loss of the lives of these men, women and children. I was surprised to find myself weeping. Maybe I was crying for myself, too, out of a newfound appreciation that life—mine and others'—is precious, precarious and only given for a time. Maybe a new place in my heart was coming into existence.

My medical emergency has helped me to understand the finiteness of my life and the need to try to live each day fully.

I'd like to say that now I wake up every morning filled with gratitude for another twenty-four hours to live, that never again will I take my heartbeat for granted. Unfortunately, that is not completely the case. Still, my medical emergency has helped me to understand the finiteness of my life and the need to try to live each day fully.

My younger daughter, Annie, used to love piggy-back rides and ask for them whenever we would be walking. Usually I would oblige gladly. Sometimes, though, when I was tired, I would say "No, not now." Invariably, she would nudge her way in front of me, throw up her arms and cry, "Before it's too late!" Her ploy worked every time. That phrase, so wise in its urgency, has come to my mind on many occasions. She was simply reminding me that soon she would be too heavy to lift, but I was hearing the more profound challenge that her exclamation suggested. How many opportunities to serve, to take delight, to grow and to make a difference have I let pass, thinking there will always be another time? The heart problems were giving me the same message as my daughter that now is the time to act. Only the present moment is given.

—

The heart attack came, not coincidentally, at the darkest time of my life. Something inconceivable was occurring: the breakdown of my marriage. The thought of divorce, especially in light of our three children, was unimaginable to me. We were not the kind of people that get divorced. Yet the persistent signs that the marriage could not be sustained despite all efforts were overwhelming. I knew for some time that my wife and I could not stay married, but just as I had ignored the chest pains until there was no way to continue, I put off acting on the divorce until remaining together became an absolute impossibility. My health crisis finally helped me face that difficult reality.

If it was hard for me to give up the illusion of myself as a perfectly healthy person when the heart problems arose, it was devastating for me to let go of my perception of myself as a perfectly good husband and father. I would have done anything to avoid facing the fact that our marriage was broken beyond repair and that my kids would not have the family life I had imagined for them. I knew what I had to do, but it took me years to do it. In this case doing the right thing did not at all feel noble or good. It was simply the necessary thing.

Whereas the heart attack seemed like an ordeal that was visited upon me, I had to accept my own responsibility in bringing about the divorce.

In getting separated and then divorced, I walked into a no man's land that I had never expected or wanted to enter. Facing that decision was the hardest thing I have ever done. It was not pretty, and it was most certainly painful. It did not fit into any ideal I had of my life as a spiritual journey. Could there be grace even in the death of a marriage that my own weakness and faults helped to bring about? Whereas the heart attack seemed like an ordeal that was visited upon me, I had to accept my own responsibility in bringing about the divorce, a "bad" thing, and that gave it a murkier and more ambiguous significance.

I wanted an intact family life for my children. It was not possible. I believe, though, that unclenched from the throes of our daily marital struggle, their mother and I have been better parents apart than we could have been together—a difficult reality, but one that needed to be faced. Only with time did I come to understand that the failure and messiness of divorce was not extraneous to my life, even if it was regrettable. Somehow, it belonged in the unfolding of my particular life. It was, to use Judith Viorst's phrase, *a necessary loss*, from which new beginnings were to emerge.

My life's path, like everyone's, has had unexpected turns. Reality can be a tough neighborhood to live in sometimes, but all the spiritual masters seem to recommend it. God is found not only on the pleasant boulevards but around every dangerous corner and down every dark alley. There is grace in illness and in the return to health, in the pain of divorce and in the ability to love again. I have learned that harsh trials and apparent good fortune are all of a piece. Kübler-Ross is right—the losses and pain are gifts. Only our capacity to accept them for what they are is in question.

Entertaining Failure

by Alice Camille

paghetti, I knew, would help. Spaghetti and cheese and lots of red sauce. I put the pot of water on to boil, but my hands were shaking. I peeled cloves of garlic and chopped red onion and let the tears splash on the counter.

The smooth dark stone surface was one of the features of this kitchen that had convinced me to take the apartment. I had lived in these very lovely rooms in the center of town for just a few months, and I would be leaving them soon. Another address. Another job. Another city.

A watched pot isn't supposed to boil, but as I stared into the water vacantly, pearl-like bubbles began to travel from the bottom to the top, releasing their cache of air at the surface. I shuddered; my chest heaved with a long-suppressed sob. I wiped my face in the towel, looked back blankly at the increasingly agitating water and said aloud: "What now?"

It is one of the accepted prerogatives of living alone that you can talk to yourself (and even answer yourself) if you have something to say that you think you ought to hear. But I wasn't ready for that conversation, not yet.

> *I started to count the usual blessings.*

I got up this morning expecting just another normal day at work. I hadn't foreseen the upheaval that would come by nightfall and was still at a loss at the turn things had taken so abruptly.

I started to count the usual blessings. I had no dependents, thank God, who would be affected by all this. No one else would be inconvenienced by another trip to Goodwill to dump a load of clothes and furniture that would not be making the move. No one else would have to share the upcoming season of uncertainty and then learn to get around another new city.

Actually, I thought, the new-city part of a move was always exciting, a time full of exquisite little discoveries: where the markets, pharmacies and hardware stores were, of course; and where's the best place to buy an emergency ice-cream cone or the funniest greeting cards; or where to take languorous strolls on sunny days. It usually didn't take me long to get a city figured out. When it came to making geographical adjustments, I was a professional.

Of course it had been apparent there was trouble at work. I knew that before I was hired. I knew that the job was not a good fit, that I was overqualified in certain respects and ruefully inexperienced in others. I had also intuited that the hiring came over my boss's head and that she hadn't really approved it. She and I didn't click from the start. We were two different people with dissimilar values and goals for the department. Also, our personalities were riotously mismatched. But I had hoped we could be civilized about these things—find ways to respect each other and maybe even learn a bit from our contrasting styles. I had even harbored the illusion that someday we might be friends and laugh when we looked back on the old wariness between us. We would have learned to be so much bigger than our differences!

I had lived too long in California, obviously. I had drunk too deeply of the gospel of personal development. I was back East now, where people were not so convinced that every conflict could end in amicable resolution. Things didn't change so fast around here, nor did opinions or patterns of behavior or people. There was no expectation that they should. This was Hester Prynne territory, where you earned your identifying letter early and wore it until it burned into your skin.

So now I was going to lose my security deposit because I had signed a year's lease on the apartment and had only lasted four months on the job. There was tension at work, for sure, but I had not anticipated *this*.

I was working my way up to naming what had happened

that afternoon, but it was still the unpronounceable *F* word: *fired*. Which led to another *F* word that made me tremble: *failed*, or worse, *failure*. I was beginning to feel like that—a failure, a person unable to retain a job or a sense of stability upon which to build a concrete identity. This would make my third involuntary termination in five years' time. I had left situation after situation in a cloud of incompletion, feeling less sure each time just what it was that I was good at. Painfully enough, I also made friends in each new setting, shared some good times with them, and then watched it all disintegrate into memories. The woman who drove me to the Greyhound station the last time was in great distress: "I have never lost a friend like this before," she declared tearfully as she embraced me.

> *I had left situation after situation in a cloud of incompletion, feeling less sure each time just what it was that I was good at.*

She had her arms around nothing; I was already miles away. "I have," I whispered.

＿

Mom says I was the only one of her babies to be born on time, on the very day I was expected. Living up to expectations was something I was born to, I guess, and initially I was quite good at it. Maybe too good. I was successful in school—not the straight-A type like my valedictorian sister, but no stranger to the honor roll. I was judged promising enough to get into the accelerated classes in high school. It was a foregone conclusion I would remain in the academic world a while longer, maybe even become a teacher or professor myself.

Grownups in general approved of me. I was not a problem to anyone, neither boisterous nor contradictory. I didn't ask the wrong questions and did what I was supposed to do. In Catholic terms, at least, I was a *good* girl.

Living up to expectations had become such a habit that I grew accustomed to succeeding. Was this bad? In college, I took a course in Epistemology, an inelegant word that refers to the theory of knowledge: how do we know what we know? It was a highly abstract brainteaser of a class, aimed at untangling the mass of assumptions that underlie the things we accept as true at face value. The textbooks were dense and the arguments hard to follow. My brain hurt trying to keep up with the classroom discussion. Still, my papers were returned to me with the word "Satisfactory" written at the top all semester. I even earned an occasional word of praise from Dr. Clay, our intellectually formidable professor.

So imagine my surprise when Dr. Clay invited me into her office near the end of the term and sat me down in the chair by her desk. "I am thinking of giving you a C for the semester," she said calmly.

I tried not to react, but the words stung like a slap. At this level of my studies, such a grade would have been devastating. "Do I deserve a C?" I asked.

She sighed. "I don't know about 'deserve,' but I think you may need one."

What I really needed was to step outside for a minute. The philosophy department seemed stuffier than usual, and the air even harder to breathe. "I don't understand," I admitted. This conversation was starting to sound more like Epistemology all the time.

Dr. Clay sat back on her chair and folded her hands carefully. "This course is all about knowing. It occurs to me you don't know how to fail. That would be a good lesson to learn, and sooner rather than later." She explained that one of *her* professors had given her an undeserved low grade once. On a transcript unsullied by so much as an A-minus, she had been humiliated by that blot of infamy and had fought to get it removed. But the professor had insisted that perfection was an addiction that would cripple her life in graduate studies and beyond if she did not come to terms with it.

"But it isn't fair!" I said. I realized I had raised my voice. It sounded shrill and a little too desperate. I didn't want to prove her point, that I was addicted to succeeding, so I regained control and lowered my voice. "I think what your professor did to you was a terrible injustice. And I want my grades to reflect the quality of my work."

When the semester came to an end and the transcript arrived, I looked at the column near Epistemology and saw the letter I had worked so long and hard for: "A." For the first time since that eerie conversation, I found that I could breathe.

Staring at the pot for several minutes, I realized the water was boiling down. I broke up some spaghetti and threw it in, stirred it with a wooden spoon and suddenly burst out laughing. "Dr. Clay," I announced to the empty kitchen, "Thanks for the warning! I have gotten my C at last."

It was true. I found failure unacceptable. I found anything less than total approval unbearable. Whether the issue was work or relationships or personal discipline, I had structured my interior world around always getting an A.

The problem was, nothing lasted.

But after college, a perfect grade was harder to come by. My professional life was fine, judging by appearances. I had glowing references from past employers, and my resume contained some attractive appointments. I interviewed well, and people seemed pleased to hire me. I got every job I went after. According to the documentation, I was a "collaborative" co-worker, a "kindly" supervisor, a "dependable and responsible" employee. Making friends didn't seem to be a problem. Nor was being flexible, meeting challenges, or riding a steep learning curve. I had never done the same job twice, but I always managed to find my footing in a new one in no time.

But the problem was, nothing lasted. Beginnings were strong; things looked promising; the crest of effort and accomplishment rose; and then, sooner or later, each situation thinned out. Always it came to this, the night of spaghetti, the need for comfort food to get past the inertia and back on the wheel of resolve and motion. Why was I here again? Why did I put out A-effort in my career over and over and come up with nothing but C's? Maybe it would be good to figure this out, once and for all, before I engaged the cycle again.

Maybe, before I took another job, I ought to stand still for a while, at least until I knew where I was going.

—

Epistemology, I hated to admit it, might be the key to unlocking the dark box of failure and seeing what was inside. I suddenly flashed on the memory of pulling the covers over my head and moaning. That was ten years earlier, back in the dormitory at college.

My roommate, Missy, had just stunned me by reporting that she was engaged to a guy I had dated the previous semester. She fluttered her diamond under my nose and danced out of the room merrily on a cloud. I plunged into bed and drew the covers over my humiliation. It had ended badly between Chuck and me. It had never been right for five minutes; but Missy made it work? Missy, who wore baby-doll pajamas with pom-pom ties and thought the definition of a thrilling weekend was watching the John Wayne film festival on television? I groaned with the hangover of shame.

My best friend Nadine arrived at my bedside faithfully as soon as the ring had made its way down the hall into her room. "Oh, you poor thing." She sat on the edge of the bed and talked to the covers. "How bad is it?"

I popped my head out and sat up in exasperation. "I don't care about Chuck!" I shouted, to make that clear. "He was pathetic. Always whining about his migraines and his parents and his Baptist morals and his grades!" I took a deep breath, and then covered my face with my hands. "But how could Missy do the one thing I couldn't do with every ounce of my strength: make him care enough to commit?"

> "The real question is: What were you doing wasting your time with Chuck to begin with?"

Nadine gazed at me sympathetically for a long time. Finally, she smoothed my hair maternally and spoke in soft tones. "You're right. You don't care about Chuck. You never did. He's right for Missy, because they both operate on the same level: Duh. But you wanted so much more from a relationship, and Chuck couldn't possibly provide you with that."

She leaned in and looked at me through mock-narrowed eyes. "The real question is: What were you doing wasting your time with Chuck to begin with? That's what *we* all want to know."

➤

I turned off the heat under the spaghetti, grabbed the potholders, and put the colander in the sink. Maybe there was a way in which I too had been operating on the level of Duh. I dumped the pasta, drained the water, and got out the good china. I even uncorked a bottle of chardonnay. Maybe I had something to celebrate tonight.

I had not wanted Chuck. That was certainly true. But losing him was something else again. And the same might be said of the last row of mystery dates I'd been on. Crashing and burning in a relationship was mighty unpleasant under any circumstances. But why had I gone out with any of these guys to begin with? Perhaps there was a correlation between the state of my resume and all those tragic-comic men who sat across from me in restaurants from Maine to California, vying for an improbable role in my future. I failed, if *failure* was the right word, because I chose the wrong partner for the dance to begin with. I did not want these well-meaning people for companions and—quite honestly now—I did not really want all these jobs I kept losing. None of them!

> *Failure was the friend who kept me from beating my head against the same old wall for much too long.*

Now, this was a true revelation: I took jobs that I didn't want, wasn't suited for, couldn't give my heart to, and then acted surprised when things came apart. I took jobs hardwired for bad endings. So maybe failure was the universe's way of making adjustments, of telling me I took the wrong turn at Albuquerque, according to the gospel of Bugs Bunny.

Failure was the friend who kept me from beating my head against the same old wall for much too long. And even though I always managed to find another wall conveniently enough, my old pal failure wouldn't let me stay there as long as I was prepared to.

I raised my glass in a silent toast. To Chuck. To all the Chucks who chucked me.

And to Dr. Clay who thought I needed a C.

And to all the employers who had hired me and fired me on my journey of self-understanding.

No, I certainly wouldn't have liked to drag kids through this maze, but I couldn't be sorry to have found my own way through it. Maybe, if I had managed to succeed at something, I would be stuck in a dim and miserable corner of the job market forever, always wishing I were somewhere and someone else.

I sat down in my lovely little kitchen and had a great plate of spaghetti. I made a promise to commit myself more thoughtfully from now on. I resolved to get comfortable with being alone, so that I didn't feel the need to jam inappropriate companions into my evenings with a shoehorn. I would find work that was meaningful and important to me, so that I could invest in it with my whole soul. I would take my heart more seriously.

Finally, after all these years, I was learning how to know what I knew. I knew that failure, the shadowy enemy that had tracked my footsteps for years, was an ally. I was grateful he had come to dinner tonight.

A Grief Spoken

by Vinita Hampton Wright

F ive years ago, I lost a baby. I'm an editor and writer by trade; I work with words all the time. But I continue to be at a loss for words when it comes to this particular loss. "Lost baby" is what I've finally decided to call this event. It was a miscarriage, a failed pregnancy, a fetus that didn't make it, a child not fully formed.

The miscarriage ended my first and only pregnancy. The details of the pregnancy itself are not important to the story I tell here. But I want to try to describe what has happened to me as a result of the miscarriage. The loss has somehow added to my fullness as a person. My life is now, oddly enough, larger than it was before this grief.

—

First of all, my faith is different now.

The pregnancy occurred during a time when I had let go of the familiar trappings of faith. For several years I had given up formal religion, worn out from trying to maintain it. My one concession was that I attended Mass with my husband most Sunday mornings. We both come from specifically non-Catholic backgrounds, and so we sat in the back of the church and stayed fairly uninvolved in congregational life. We were content to worship rather anonymously and hoped to heal from our respective religious pasts.

I took nothing for granted and allowed myself only a bit of joy every day that my body seemed steadfastly on its course.

When I became pregnant, the first ultrasound was perfect, showing everything in the right place and as it should be for week five. Jim and I decided to wait until week twelve before informing friends and family. We knew that because of my age my chances for miscarriage were thirty to forty percent. And so I took nothing for granted and allowed myself only a bit of joy every day that my body seemed steadfastly on its course.

The second ultrasound was disappointing. The doctors had hoped to pick up a heartbeat, but there was none. But it was early, and they said that the next week would be more telling. The next week in fact showed a visible, slow heartbeat, too faint to pick up on the audio monitor. The following week, they said, would be conclusive.

I walked around that week in a daze between worried yearning and protective indifference.

That Sunday was Mother's Day. At the end of the church service, the priest asked all the mothers and mothers-to-be to stand. Jim nudged me when I hesitated. I felt weightless for that moment or two, standing up in the congregation as a mother, not knowing if my motherhood would even hold its child.

Jim took me out for Greek food, and the host greeted me with a rose—because I was a female and it was Mother's Day, I suppose. Then the waitress asked if I was a mother. I said we were expecting, and she asked when I was due. Early December, I told her.

That week, the fourth ultrasound revealed a fetus far too small, with a heart that had stopped beating altogether. Now all that was left for Jim and me was the waiting for our dead baby to actually miscarry, which could take anywhere from a day to weeks.

On the Sundays that fell within that horrible period, we went to Mass. Every Sunday I knelt and held my palms up, physically or mentally, and said to God, "I give this situation to you. Help me accept whatever happens." I didn't beg or bargain. I didn't plead or threaten or mutter. I discovered that after years of not having much faith at all I now had faith that allowed me to pray this calm prayer. Something inside was suddenly strong and confident enough in God's love that I could pray these words with integrity.

I had done nothing to generate this faith, nothing to work

up to it. Faith just sort of appeared and took up residence in my soul.

—

How does one carry with love a dead child-to-be? What grief is appropriate? I prayed and hoped that the miscarriage would happen within the week. I actually made a trip to my mother and extended family in Kansas to attend some high-school graduations, knowing full well that this womb death could happen at any time. My husband, meanwhile, was helping his oldest son move across the country, a trip that had been planned months before.

> *As it turned out, I lost the baby alone at home—a long evening of hurting and pacing and bleeding and giving up.*

As it turned out, I lost the baby alone at home—a long evening of hurting and pacing and bleeding and giving up. My body expelled the small sac, and I put it in water in a dish and placed the dish carefully in the refrigerator. I wrapped myself in a robe, made some hot tea, and waited for Jim to call from the road, as he did every evening. He called and I gave him our news. We sorrowed together for a few moments, but I was tired and couldn't talk long. The next two days, before Jim returned, a friend stayed with me.

Jim and I went to church the following Sunday. I cried

only once, toward the beginning of the service. But I was able to kneel—as I had for weeks, during all of the hoping and trying and dreading—and say, "God, my hands are open. Help me receive all parts of my life as gifts from you." I found I was still able to make that prayer. Not only that, I was able to smile at mothers of young children without feeling attacked by their happiness.

Since those dark days, in fact, I have not had to work desperately at faith, as I had for so many years before. I trust God to watch over me, regardless of my mental or emotional state. I realize that relinquishing my own frenetic and feverish activity can be a good thing.

———

The second transformation this loss brought to my life is that I discovered a wound in the Body of Christ.

The Monday after I lost the baby was Memorial Day. Jim and I sat on the couch and discussed what to do with the unfinished child in the dish in the refrigerator. We live on the third floor of a six-flat in Chicago; there is no yard for burial. We thought of burning the dead fetus and doing something with the ashes, but it had been in water for several days and we felt the need to do something right away. We decided to deliver our child to the waters of Lake Michigan, barely a mile from our home.

For the first time, I sobbed without hope. The thought of not having my lost baby close by brought fresh panic and grief.

For the first time, Jim looked at the fetus. I showed him the bloody strand at one end that would have become the umbilical chord. I picked up the sac and let it roll this way and that, revealing through the translucent membranes the tiny dark organs that had begun to form.

We drained the water and put the sac in a jar, the jar in a paper sack. We drove to the lakefront, where so many families and couples were arriving to cook and watch the waves and throw balls or Frisbees. A high sun warmed the near-chilly wind. We walked out to a point where no one swims and climbed down to the cement ledge nearest the water. The waves were still rough enough that much of the ledge was wet. Sun sparkles rolled over the green water like sequins.

While Jim held my left hand, I took the tiny sac in my right. It weighed hardly anything at all. I threw it far enough that it would sink rather than wash back onto the rocks at our feet. It lingered only a few seconds on the surface, and then it sank from sight.

—

It was, at least by medical standards, an uneventful miscarriage—no trips to the emergency room, no great hemorrhaging. In a way, I felt cheated. I wrote to a friend, "When I consider what I have lost, I think that there was far too little blood. I should have nearly bled to death. I should have been weak from the loss. But it was nothing more than a long and complicated menstrual cycle."

As the weeks went by, I found myself crying at odd times. I would suddenly feel extremely lonely for that part of myself that had been lost. I longed to see the face and form of the child (a girl, I liked to imagine) who tried so hard to be born.

I had generally held a pro-life position for years, but now the questions were pointedly specific for me.

I wondered aloud to Jim one night if there will be a daughter waiting for us in heaven, waiting to be seen for the first time, waiting for us to finally give her a name.

And I found myself asking theological and scientific questions. I had generally held a pro-life position for years, but now the questions were pointedly specific for me. When *does* the egg become a soul? When the sperm and egg meet? When the egg successfully implants in the uterine lining (this happens for only about fifty percent of fertilized eggs)? When all the organs and essential features are formed? When the heart starts? Once the heart has started, however weakly, does that mean that when it stops there should be a funeral? I needed to know what exactly it was that I had lost. I needed instruction in how to mourn.

If all that had left me was mere failed tissue, shouldn't I have felt better before too long, as if my body had gone through a short illness? Instead, I felt that I had experienced a death—a real death that mattered, if only to Jim and me.

As an editor in religious publishing, I've followed at a distance theological debates and definitions. Yet in this area, where theologians could be completely relevant, I'm not sure they're much help. I think the church has dealt with miscarriage by not dealing with it.

It's not that I mind if our ministers come up with no clear answers, but I'd like to know that they are at least in the struggle with us—those women who deal with this particular loss.

Why has there never been a religious ritual developed for the woman who could not produce a healthy birth? Why are there no liturgies for the children who left before we could get to know them? Why did Jim and I have to have our own burial service on the shore of Lake Michigan?

The argument of so many religious people against abortion is that the fetus in formation is very much a soul. If abortion is the taking of human life, then why is that same life not acknowledged as such when it departs through miscarriage?

I've been amazed to learn how many women have been through miscarriage multiple times.

I think it is simply that religious professionals are afraid of this topic. The fear begets silence, and the silence infects us all—even the men and women who are in the midst of suffering. The few times I have mentioned my lost baby, at least one woman present has been quick to tell me that she had one too. I've been amazed to learn how many women have been through miscarriage *multiple* times. Yet we've been trained not to talk about it, because no one knows what to do with our sorrow.

—

Jim and I managed a miscarriage, if that is really possible. We made our own sort of burial. We grieved together. But then I discovered that I still had a life in front of me but had no passion for living it.

I could think of nothing to look forward to. I felt empty and ended. I went to work in the morning and somehow got through the day. I would look forward to Jim's hugs in the evening, but nothing between one of his hugs and the next held any interest for me.

Sometimes I would try to think of our loss as an insignificant thing. It happens to so many women, after all. It wasn't even a fully formed person but a configuration of organs that were unable to keep going—a small purse of gray membrane that slipped out of me so easily that it was but a momentary, slick sensation.

I had been only nine weeks pregnant. And now I was walking and talking like a normal person. I rode the train and worked in my office. I laughed with people and cooked dinner. I cooed and grinned over other people's babies. How could such a small thing engulf me so?

Yet part of me knew that I should mourn, knew that what had happened was a major life event. Although we informed our families, I received no cards or letters from them that acknowledged I had lost anything, and the only phone call I received was from my sister.

I have good women friends, and they have been attentive to my very real loss. But a woman who does not produce a living child should not expect to keep a scrapbook of remembrances. There is no funeral, no line of mourners gathered and waiting to offer words of condolence. She and her husband, if they have no other children, will never be seen as parents in any real sense.

The Body of Christ contains many wounds, and this is one of them: mothers and fathers who lose their unborn children, the faces of whom they never see, the bodies of whom they never embrace.

And so I can now pray, "Lord Jesus Christ, the great bearer of our sorrows and wounds, I am better acquainted with you now. I am drawn close to all the others like me who are also a part of you."

—

A third good change is my life is that I have become more connected to the world of human beings.

Like any other grief, this one is never really over. It has a life of its own, and that became apparent as, eventually, my emotions began to reach down and grab hold of the event. Weeks after the miscarriage, I was palpably missing the child I would have had. I began feeling the twinges of pain at more levels and more frequently throughout the day.

And there are those silent anniversaries that others never see. The heart remembers vividly; the body does too. Jim and I commemorated the two-year mark of our lost baby by throwing two pale roses into the waters where we had performed the burial. And my body heaved and sobbed as if I had lost the child that very day. I had expected it to be a somber event, but the physical hysteria was a shock to me.

I realized that I had become part of something much bigger in a way I couldn't control. This little bit of "tissue" had reattached me to the world. In my initial grief I had preferred seclusion, silence, and as little to do with physical life as possible. But an embryo, however young and malformed, had resided in my body for a few weeks and had exhibited a heartbeat, however faint. I found that I could not ignore this fact. My body had expelled that piece of tissue, and then I had flung it into the lake on a windy afternoon. I didn't know I was throwing anchor. By that tiny strand of life I have become lashed to all life, to our common humanity.

> *By that tiny strand of life I have become lashed to all life.*

My lost baby's presence will never be undone. It has become a shadow just over my shoulder, a slight, constant humming near my ear. It is a waft of extra joy, of additional pain, pressing on my heart.

You're not the same once you've conceived. You're not even the same once you've tried. By that very act you are joined in another way to the great human enterprise. You've made a choice to be touched by something outside yourself, offered yourself to the whole realm of persons—past, present and future. Who knows what the response will be—and what that response will do to you?

I have not conceived again, but the risking itself has accomplished something.

It is a wonderful thing that I have risked myself since then again and again for the sake of bearing a child. I have not conceived again, but the risking itself has accomplished something—added wisdom perhaps, or courage, or simply the sense that I am not alone.

—

One morning, a couple of weeks after the miscarriage, I sat on our porch. It was a soft morning and cool enough that my robe felt warm and good. In those days I drank red wine in the mornings, even before work, just a little glass in the airy daylight before the real day began. That morning I had my glass of wine and ate some crackers. I read a chapter from a book that had nothing to do with my life.

It occurred to me then that I was wearing a pink terry robe. And I remembered suddenly a photo taken of my mother when she was in her thirties. Her hair was longer than it had been most of my childhood. She looked different from her usual self, sitting on a chair in the living room, smiling at the camera. And she wore a pink terry robe. It was shortly after her return from the hospital. She had had a miscarriage, a lost child that occurred between my two younger sisters. My mother is a storyteller, but her recounting of that incident has always been brief. Mainly, she remembers the hemorrhaging and the frantic drive to the emergency room. She recalls my father helping the orderly afterwards to look through the mess in the floorboards. They never found the fetus.

I sipped wine in the gentle morning, in my pink robe, and thought of my mother decades ago, bleeding also, in pink.

Our grief is never merely our own. It is the ancient grief, turned over and over throughout the galaxies and the generations. This grief grabs you up and spills you at the door of the universe. Or it opens its arms, and when you fall into them you find the rest of the world there too.

Like Setting Fire to a Fifty-Dollar Bill

by Patrick T. Reardon

I walk out the door of my suburban newspaper office, out to the parking lot, into the harsh sunlight of dusk on an early Friday evening. It's been a long day. It's been a long summer and autumn. I'm drained and want nothing more than to get in my car and head back into Chicago, to my empty apartment, for a supper of carefully calibrated proportions and a night of whatever's on television.

The year is 1981. It's late October. I'm dieting. I've lost forty pounds in the last four months. I don't eat desserts or anything else made with processed sugar. I've quit cigarettes. I've given up caffeinated coffee. I feel like a monk or, more accurately, a prisoner, living a circumscribed existence dictated by my body's confusing signals of distress and my doctor's grasping for answers.

At this moment, though, I have to make a choice. A few weeks earlier, I signed up for a retreat that my parish, Saint Clement, is sponsoring for single people. Saint Clement is in a former working-class area of the city, now undergoing gentrification. The parish roster is heavy with young, unmarried men and women like me, building careers and gingerly trying to figure out our place in a world completely different from the one our mothers and fathers found upon entering adulthood. Our parents, even the ones who served in World War II, married early and started having children early. It gave their lives solidity. They were firmly rooted. We, though, are the initial wave of a generation that—because of the women's movement, the sexual revolution, and our own fascination with freedom—has been slow to settle down. We are pioneers, exploring what life holds for those who don't take the early road to matrimony. You could call us overgrown children—and there are those who do. But we're also pathfinders, blazing a trail through a new cultural landscape.

> *We have control of our lives, but we have no one to share them with.*

Many critics of my generation are jealous of our freedoms. That's understandable. But there's a flipside to that liberty. Most of us, as we scramble up the ladders of work worlds and sample the wide variety of pleasures and amusements, are—when we go home at night—just plain lonely.

We have control of our lives, but we have no one to share them with. We're keeping our options open, and that means we're hanging out in space, unconnected, apart, alone.

So Saint Clement has been beefing up its programs for unmarried parishioners. There's the folk Mass on Sunday mornings in the basement of the church. There are discussion groups that meet weekly or monthly, and picnics and parties galore. More to the point of this story, there is the annual weekend retreat, held at a monastery, far out from the city, amid the cows and cornfields at the distant edge of the suburban subdivisions.

I've never signed up for the retreat before. Although I go to the folk Mass on Sundays, I haven't locked into any of the other activities the way so many single men and women in the parish have. They have turned the parish into something like a small town, where they know everyone and everyone knows them. I, however, sit by myself in my usual spot in the back of the pews to the right of the altar, behind the guitarists and singers. I watch the smiles and hugs and kisses, the bright eyes with which they greet each other, and I feel like I'm in some other world. It's as if they know a secret language that I'm too stupid or too proud to learn.

But after much hesitation I've made an initial—if ever-so-tentative—move to take a dive into the parish social stream. In a moment of weakness (or perhaps loneliness), I filled out an application for the retreat and plunked down fifty dollars (which meant a lot more to me then than it would now) for the weekend.

That fifty dollars is the key to this story.

Sending in the application and money had been an impulsive decision a couple weeks earlier. I'd been changing so much about my life that going on my first singles' retreat seemed to fit right in. A few months earlier, I'd woken up achy and sweaty and dizzy. I couldn't seem to focus my eyes very well. I had to concentrate greatly just to walk to the bathroom. A bad case of the flu, I figured; it would go away. But it didn't go away.

Suddenly, at age thirty-one, after a lifetime of robust good health, I was sick, ill with a mystery ailment that had my doctor flummoxed. I had no energy. I felt overwhelmed, crushed. And the doctor's inability to name, much less treat my illness made me feel worse. At home in my apartment, alone, weighed down and empty, I thought how much simpler and less scary it would have been if I'd just broken my leg. A broken leg seemed, in that topsy-turvy moment, like a blessing I'd been denied.

Test after test failed to pinpoint the reason I felt so lousy.

Test after test failed to pinpoint the reason I felt so lousy. So my doctor began to attack the problem on several fronts, hoping that one of the strategies or the combination of them all would do the job.

First, he had the dietitian in his practice work with me to teach me to eat smaller, better-balanced meals and develop a regular exercise regime in order to lose weight and tone up my body. She gave me a paperback book, listing the calories of thousands of foods, including the entire array of McDonald's cuisine, and showed me how to keep track of my daily calorie intake.

This has meant quite a lifestyle change for me. As a single guy, I used to eat a lot of fast food. I ordered a lot of pizzas. A good meal in my own kitchen was a large steak, a box or two of Kraft macaroni and cheese, and several glasses of Coke or Pepsi—with the greater part of a box of chocolate doughnuts for dessert.

These days, however, supper is usually a grilled breast of skinless, boneless chicken, a small salad with red wine vinegar instead of dressing, and a serving of peas or green beans or corn. I drink only one glass of milk (skim, of course) with maybe an apple to top off the meal.

One of the tests I took showed that my body isn't handling glucose very well—taking it in too quickly and getting rid of it faster than normal. So my doctor has advised me to avoid processed sugar. Fruit and other naturally sweet foods are fine; so are artificial sweeteners such as aspartame. But anything with refined sugar, corn syrup and their many permutations is *verboten*.

Caffeine, my doctor said, also has an impact on glucose levels, so I've switched to decaf coffee and caffeine-free pop. In line with another of his suggestions, I've smoked my last cigarette—quitting at midnight on September 15, thirty-eight days ago (but who's counting).

I now stand in this near-empty parking lot, considering this choice: Do I drive the hour or more along crowded suburban highways to get to the retreat, or do I simply head for home?

I've been rigorous in carrying out these lifestyle changes because I've been so scared by my illness. In a part of my mind, I approached these new ways of living as if I were a rookie at spring training or a new recruit at boot camp. I put myself into the hands of my doctor and his dietitian, hoping—believing—that if I followed their guidelines I'd feel better.

And that's what has happened. I have slowly started feeling better. About two weeks after the onset of the ailment, I was able to go back to work. Working out three days a week at the local health club, I now feel stronger and more fit than I have since high school.

I'm still hungry a lot, although much less than at first, now that my stomach and appetite have shrunk. I still miss real coffee; decaf is like drinking hot, colored water. And cigarettes—well, let's just say I'm chewing a lot of (sugarless) gum. But I am more aware of my body and of the world around me. I feel once again the snap, crackle and pop of life.

I've slowed down. I'm not racing on a sugar-and-caffeine high anymore. At work I'm a little less frantic about getting things done quickly. I've risked changing, and the changes—for all their bumps and pains—have been good.

So here I stand in the parking lot, facing yet one more change.

It was easy a couple of weeks ago to say to myself that, yeah, I was ready to take the plunge and go on this retreat. The brochure promised a mix of praying and partying. I felt I was ready to get to know some of the other single men and women in the parish. I was willing to throw myself into the sort of social situation I usually abhor—the kind in which I'm expected to introduce myself to total strangers, to make small talk, to act like I'm having a good time, to endure the acute embarrassment of putting myself in the social spotlight.

To spend money frivolously—to not get your money's worth—was right up there with the other serious sins.

At this particular moment, however, I find that I have little desire or energy to follow through on that commitment. It would be easy to chuck the idea and just drive for home. No one would miss me. They don't even know that I exist.

It's so tempting, and I'm just about to do it when I realize that if I skip the retreat I'll be wasting my fifty dollars.

You see, I was raised in an extremely frugal family. We never wasted *anything*. My parents grew up during the Great Depression, and they instilled in my siblings and me an almost pathological respect for the value of money and the need to use it wisely. To spend money frivolously—to not get your money's worth—was right up there with the other serious sins.

To skip the retreat would be like taking a fifty-dollar bill and setting it on fire.

So I go to the retreat. I feel terribly uncomfortable at first, but I meet a few people, including one red-haired woman with a slight gap in her front teeth and the liveliest eyes I've ever seen. She, too, has been knocked out of her rhythm in recent months by breaking her right leg sliding into first base. (When we talk later, she admits that she had been trying to show off.) Her leg is still in an ankle-to-thigh cast, and she is on crutches. But at the first evening party, when the music is loud and I am standing, as usual, along one of the walls, there she is, out on the dance floor. She is dancing, sort of. Really she is just jumping up and down on her uninjured left foot, whooping loudly, with a smile as broad as all life.

Exactly one year and one week later, we marry.

And now, two decades later, my time before we met seems like someone else's life.

Our two teenage children continue to be fascinated by the details of the story of our meeting. What if I hadn't gotten sick? What if Cathy hadn't broken her leg? Most of all, what if their old man hadn't been so horrified at the thought of wasting fifty dollars that he had headed home for bed instead of dragging himself to the retreat?

For them, the slightest of variation on this story could have meant that they would never have been born.

The same is true for me.

The Language of God

by James (Jeff) Behrens

My twin, Jimmy, whose name I took when I entered the Trappist monastery, was eighteen years old when he was killed in a car accident. The accident took place on Saturday May 29th, 1966. He died early the next morning. Both Jimmy and I would have been eighteen years old on the 31st, and that day was spent in the funeral home.

Before he died, Jimmy underwent several surgeries. He was dying from massive internal injuries, and the doctor asked me if I would give blood in the hope that my blood might congeal with my brother's more readily than that of others. It did not work. Jimmy died, and he did so with some of me in him.

I like to think that not all of my last gift to him was drained out of his body. Something of what was once me may yet rest in his body in the grave, even if it has now turned to dust with the rest of him. We are bonded for eternity, in a cemetery in northern New Jersey.

James (Jeff) Behrens   125

The days around Jimmy's death were very painful for me. I was probably in a state of shock. I cannot recall many things—the funeral Mass, the cemetery service, the people coming to the house. Other things I do remember as clear as if they happened yesterday. I remember visiting Jimmy's wrecked car an hour or so after it hit the tree. I remember giving the blood, staring at it as it flowed into a glass tube. I remember seeing the cab with Mom and Dad arriving at the hospital (for they had been away in New Orleans when the accident happened). I remember seeing them cry when the doctor told them that "Jimmy did not make it." The doctor was crying too.

"All you go through, loving and raising a son, and in one night he is gone," he said, more sorrowfully than I thought was humanly possible.

Most of all, I remember a walk with my dad on the afternoon after Jimmy died. We walked around the block slowly, as if we were dragging a great weight on our shoulders. He asked me if I thought Jimmy knew that his parents loved him. (Jimmy had gotten himself into a bit of trouble a few weeks earlier.) I told Dad that we both knew that he and Mom loved us very much. He started to cry. "All you go through, loving and raising a son, and in one night he is gone," he said, more sorrowfully than I thought was humanly possible.

I remember those words and the way he said them and his crying as we walked. But then he said, "Jeff, is there anything Mama and I can do for you? Is there anything at all?" It turned out that Dad was worried about *me*. I told him I was okay and that we would all get through it.

But the truth is that I did not know whether we would get through it or not, much less how.

———

Years later, another man asked me from the grief of his heart, "Jeff, is there anything I can do for you?"

His name was Ron, and he had been crying too. Several days before, early in the morning, his wife, Kathy, had called me. As soon as I heard her voice, I knew that their daughter Denise, a forty-one-year-old mother of two little boys, had died. Denise had been sick for some months. Kathy and I both cried on the phone, and I blurted out, "Is there anything I can do for you and Ron, anything at all?"

Kathy asked that I come and stay with them at their home. They wanted me to be with them during the wake and say the funeral Mass.

Of course I went, and so a couple of days later I found myself at their home. It was evening and Kathy had gone off to bed exhausted. Ron and I sat at the kitchen table. In a broken-hearted voice, he looked at me and said in a tone that reminded me of my dad's that day so many years before, "Jeff, we prayed and prayed. We did all we could for Denise,

James (Jeff) Behrens   127 and then we prayed some more. It was all so useless. All for nothing. She's gone, and nothing could have prevented her death."

He paused a moment and lowered his head, and before I could say anything he looked at me again and said, "Jeff, what do you need? Is there anything we can do for you?"

I looked at him in amazement. His words meant more to me than he realized. They recalled almost word for word the sad offer made by my father from his grief to my grief, over thirty-six years before.

I looked at Ron and said, "No, Ron. I'm okay. Really, I am doing okay." He smiled sorrowfully and said, "Good."

What I suddenly realized—it was as if scales had actually fallen from my eyes—was that the human instinct to reach out and give and help one another is stronger and far more powerful than death. Indeed, it is experiencing the death of what we love most that gives birth to a deep, loving goodness that allows us to transcend our own needs and desires. It is death itself that opens us up and allows us to be whatever we can for each other.

How is it that we speak words that come from the very spirit of God who is in us, while moments before we spoke of the uselessness of our prayers and efforts to love? We despair in our grief, yet almost in the same breath we redirect our hearts to the needs of those we love? We "speak" for

God, even as we cry over not having been rescued from the pain of the death of a loved one.

"Is there anything I can do for you?" Dad asked in his sorrow. "Is there anything I can do for you?" Ron asked in his.

———

Mom tells me that Jimmy and I chatted with each other when we were still in the crib together. It was not English, though. It was some kind of baby talk. She watched us and tells me that we seemed to understand each other. Of course, I remember none of that.

The more commonly shared language of English soon grabbed our fancies, however, and the larger world slowly but surely came to Jimmy and me—word by word, image by image. But after Jimmy died, I was on my own in reaching out to this world and trying to understand it, to know for sure what that Presence is that surrounds me and is within me and those I love.

After Jimmy died, I was on my own in reaching out to this world and trying to understand it.

Sometimes it is painful to share myself with another human being. It can hurt to be that vulnerable. But I know that love opens me to another. And so does pain. And so does death.

Pain exacts a language from us. Some pain, like an everyday misunderstanding, is easy enough to heal with the language we normally speak, or with the language of a kiss or a hug. But there are far deeper pains that wound us so deeply we are never the same again. The loss of a son or daughter, a brother or sister, a mother or father, a husband or wife, a child or dear friend—no human language, no human gesture of comfort can assuage that pain. It breaks us, but that very breaking opens us to something we cannot of ourselves provide for each other.

> *I knew that God was and is a living part of their pain, my pain, our pain.*

It is only after we open ourselves through the very rupture of our very being (that includes, perhaps, even articulation of some very human anger or despair) that we can ask, wondrously, if there is anything we can "do" for one another.

At Denise's funeral, I remember standing at the altar, saying as I had said many thousands of times before the words of consecration. Just in front of me knelt Ron and Kathy and Gerald, Denise's husband, her sister, Mary Beth, and her brother, Al. They were crying. I looked down at the sacred words and at the vessels and the bread and wine. I knew that God was and is a living part of their pain, my pain, our pain.

Sometime during that Mass I looked at Denise's husband and at their little boys and at Ron and Kathy. I thought of the vows of marriage: "for better, for worse; for richer, for poorer; in sickness and in health; until death do us part." These words are part of the divine language we need to comprehend our very nature, to bond with each other for a lifetime—and beyond—of lasting love. They are the words that help us find a place in life where we can remain with the ones we love, even after they die.

—

Jimmy and I moved from our own language to the language of the larger world—and in doing so took a good part of that world to ourselves. As we humans move from our own language to the language of God, we learn how to articulate the mysteries of life, the mysteries of sharing and sacrifice. It is the "stuff" of the vows we make to each other: bonding, community, truthfulness, patience, fidelity, endurance.

How do we learn such language? The lessons are not very far away. They are as close as the sharing of a broken heart, as close as the words of my father on a walk after my brother's death, as close as the words that were spoken to me by another father from across a kitchen table after the death of his daughter.

The meaning of it all, the gift at the heart of the universe, the "sense" of the deaths of Jimmy and Denise and all our loved ones is somehow disclosed in the simple question: "Is there anything I can do for you?"

The Gift My Brother Gave Me

by Joyce Rupp

It was mid-August of 1967. I was standing at the kitchen sink washing sticky cookie dough off my fingers when I heard the phone ring. I didn't pay much attention to the sound, as I knew one of the other three women in the house would answer it. I was busy making chocolate-chip cookies on a Saturday morning, happy to be free for one more weekend before my second year of teaching erupted into a merciless whirlwind of activity. The cookies were all neatly lined up in fresh little clumps on the baking tray, just like my mother had taught me so many years ago—a pattern of four clumps of dough, then three, then four, until the tray is full. They bake evenly that way, with just enough space in between, she explained.

Dolores came into the kitchen with the news that the phone call was for me: "It's long distance, Joyce." At those words my heart leapt. In those days, I never got a long distance call unless there was something urgent. I didn't have much time to think though. The phone was only one room away, and I was in there in just a few steps.

I picked up the receiver and had barely said "hello" when I heard my older sister's voice. It was filled with sadness: "Oh, Joyce, I am so sorry to tell you. Dave drowned in a fishing accident this morning." Her words landed like a thud on my soul. Dave? Our brother? Not Dave! He was only twenty-three years old. It just couldn't be true. I was standing there fresh, alive, full of youth, and Dave was two years younger than I. Dead? No, it couldn't be true.

I wanted to call my sister back and beg, "Tell me, please tell me you didn't mean it; that it's all a horrible mistake."

But it was. As I heard my sister's voice describing the details of the drowning, I couldn't deny the horrible reality.

I hung up the phone and stood there, emotionally paralyzed, stunned with the news. I wanted to scream, but nothing came out. I wanted to call my sister back and beg, "Tell me, please tell me you didn't mean it, that it's all a horrible mistake."

Then the paralysis ceased and huge sobs came forth—deep and uncontrollable. Dolores heard me and came and put her arms around me. She tried to comfort me, but there was no comfort to be found. I had never dreamt that one of my siblings might die—maybe our parents one day, but not a sibling, not a young man in his prime, not a brother who was supposed to have so many years ahead of him.

A great dark cloud of unrelenting sorrow engulfed me at that moment, a cloud that circled around my heart for a long, long time. I went home for the funeral and felt the weight of my parents' and siblings' anguish as well. There was little being written in the late 1960s on the topic of grief, and none of us knew how to comfort one another. We all tried to be strong, to hold back our tears. We avoided talking about how devastated we were by Dave's death. We sat silently and kept our gut-wrenching pain to ourselves, numbed with loss, unable to acknowledge how greatly each of us was hurting.

It wasn't just sorrow that I felt from my brother's death, however. There was something else snarling around in my loss. I kept hearing a huge voice of guilt. It stayed with me through the funeral. It haunted me as I returned to my teaching. It grabbed me in the dark of night and kept me awake. It clutched at my spirit and wouldn't let me go. It shook me with its clawing hands and taunted me: "You are never, never going to be at peace."

My guilt arose from our high-school days together. After his death, whenever I tried to think about Dave as a youth I couldn't remember any joyful times we might have had. Only the negative ones. I was a junior when Dave was a freshman. I was the one with the driver's license, so I drove the two of us the six miles to school every day and to any evening activities. I treated my brother like a slave those two years, wielding power over him, making him push my car out of the snow, having him beg me to take him to social events, chiding him for his stupidity, and rarely affirming him for anything he did or was.

How I longed to talk with him, to tell him how much I loved him.

When I couldn't stand this memory any longer, I turned to thinking about our time together as young adults. This only added to the pain. I had left home after a year of college to enter the convent, and Dave had joined the army after he graduated from high school. He was stationed in Germany for several years. We had little communication during that time because of the distance and the strict rules my religious community had about writing letters.

As I thought about Dave in his early twenties, I could see the living room where a group of us had last gathered, just a few months before he died. I pictured him on the sofa where he was sitting the final time I had been able to visit with him. I recalled looking over at him, thinking what a kind-hearted person he was, and feeling happy to be there with him. I remembered wishing we had some time to talk by ourselves. I wanted to tell him I was sorry for how I had acted in high school. But now I didn't have a chance to do any of that. How I longed to talk with him, to tell him how much I loved him, to beg his forgiveness for the haughtiness and cold-hearted ways of my youth.

This dark cloud of guilt and sorrow wouldn't leave me. I

felt I had no one to talk to about it. I had no close friends at that time, no confidant, no spiritual guide. Vatican II had only just concluded, and my community was slow in responding to the changes it initiated. I still was not supposed to have any close friendships with people outside my community. I lived with three other Catholic sisters who were much older than myself, and in those days we never spoke in the convent about personal issues. I knew my sisters were aware that I was hurting, and they did all they could to be kind, but I was too tightly closed to share my heart's burden with them. I wasn't willing to risk being vulnerable by disclosing my pain to someone else, even though it was so great I feared I couldn't bear it.

One day, in the midst of my heartache, I was walking back to the convent after school when I noticed a small wooded area in the distance. The convent was in a newly developed suburb and very few houses had yet been built. I had seen the two acres of trees before. They were just beyond an open field bordering the school building that the children often used as a playground.

Something inside urged me to walk over and see what the patch of woods held. Once I got there I meandered through the tall oaks and thin, bending willows, trying not to get snagged on the underbrush. I walked more and more slowly, feeling a hushed resonance. A sense of beauty and solitude came over me. The sunlight filtering through the leaves created a calming presence. The verdant foliage permeated the air with an aroma of freshness. For a moment, a tiny slit of sunlight making its way through the trees beamed something blessed into my heart—a warm ray of comfort, a brief cessation of the pain I had been bearing.

Then the experience was gone. But the door to something other than sorrow had opened for me. I knew I would come back to that spot again and again, because I sensed it held what I needed.

—

Whenever I returned to my sanctuary, I took a notebook with me. I wasn't accustomed to writing at that time. I had never heard of the spiritual practice of journaling, and although I enjoyed jotting a few poetic words now and then, being a published writer was not on my radar screen. I just had this sense that I ought to be sitting in those woods and that I ought to be writing as I did so. It was as simple and full of mystery as that.

It wasn't easy. I didn't have words for the pain inside of me. But I started to write anyhow. At first I just scribbled my observations about the external surroundings: trees, birds, weeds, sunlight, that sort of thing. Gradually I moved into including some of my reflections from my meditations on scripture and writing some brief prayers. Finally but hesitantly, I ventured into the vulnerable place of looking inside of "me." I began to write down words for the undulating agony inside of me that never seemed to go away. This led me to listen to other dimensions of my life: my loneliness, my strong need for emotional privacy, my fear of failure as a young teacher, my struggle with life that seemed to be undefined yet stretched beyond the grief of my brother's death.

One day as I sat in my woods leaning against a rough-barked oak tree, I found the courage to ask myself deeper questions.

One day as I sat in my woods leaning against a rough-barked oak tree, I found the courage to ask myself deeper questions. Who was I and whom did I want to become? What was it that I longed for in the deepest recesses of my soul? Was my life the one I honestly wanted? I came back to such challenging thoughts many times. My notebook didn't hold a lot of answers when I considered these questions, but I did feel a sense of satisfaction at being able to ask them. I was grateful for being on a journey that felt like I was coming home to a truer part of myself.

In the midst of this regular sojourning in the woods, a sense of God's hidden presence returned. It was at this time that steady little whispers of hope also slipped into my spirit. I started believing in my growth, trusting that the way would open for me to become the person I was meant to be. In fact, it was during those two years, when I sat in the woods for hours at a time, that I developed the habit of praying this small petition each day: "God, help me to become the woman you desire me to be."

—

It wasn't until fifteen years later, at a thirty-day retreat, that I was able to fully let go of my sorrow over Dave's death and my guilt about how I'd treated him. Having learned from my days in the woods to value the practice of journaling and the power that taking time for reflection can hold, I wrote a dialogue with my brother.

I told Dave of my endless sense of guilt. I apologized to him. I asked for his forgiveness. In response I heard him say to me: "You silly girl. Of course I have forgiven you, Joyce. We were just young kids. I always knew you loved me. Why are you hanging on to this old stuff? I never blamed you for what you did. I love you far too much for that. It's time you got on with your life."

> And so I did get on with my life, in ways that astounded me.

And so I did get on with my life, in ways that astounded me. Not long after that retreat I wrote my first book, which has led to an unexpected but fulfilling career. But that's not the gift my brother gave me—at least not the one I most cherish. What he gave is the best gift anyone can give. He gave me the gift of my self. Dave's death helped me find a way to go inward, to discover the healing power of nature and solitude, to open up my mind and heart so I could discover and claim my fullness and wholeness.

My brother's death served as an immense catalyst of personal transformation. It took me deep into territory I had never before traveled and perhaps never would have. It gave me courage to face questions that took me years to answer. It helped me discover and accept both my strengths and my weaknesses. It led me to discover a divine Companion who is always for me and never against me. Through the journal keeping and personal reflection that came during my grief, I found a way to be at peace no matter how upsetting and full of turmoil my outer world might be.

Grieving the devastating loss of Dave's death gave me the blessing of learning how to live with myself. It gave me confidence to enter my inner terrain. It is a blessing that continues to influence me every day of my life. I never wanted my brother to die, nor would I ever have chosen this path to come to self-revelation and growth. But it was the gift that Dave gave to me, and I would be ungrateful indeed if I did not treasure it.

Where Eagles Soar

by Joni Woelfel

It was still dark as my husband and I drove beyond a rise that dropped into the Minnesota River Valley. From there we could see for miles as the faint blush of a golden sunrise illuminated the edges of the horizon. Heavy mists lay in tendrils along the treetops, and the world seemed primeval and enveloped in shadows.

Gazing through the pickup window, I had a feeling of time and space overlapping—with night and morning both simultaneously present as I glimpsed snatches of the large white moon reflected in still, swampy pools along the roadside.

I had a blanket tucked up to my chin as my husband glanced at me, asking sympathetically, "How are you feeling?"

"Too sick to talk."

He nodded, patting the blanket as we continued on in silence. I blearily turned my attention back to the surreal, passing landscape while a longing voiced itself within as I thought of our son who had died. "Oh, Mic," I prayed, "please give me a sign to let me know you're still with us. Let me see an eagle soar."

The eagle is a universal sign of the Great Spirit and soaring freedom, associated with courage, strength and might. Native Americans felt that to see one is always a privilege and great gift. So with a heart filled with great desire but little expectation, I continued to watch for one as we passed though the valley. When we arrived at the other side, however, I knew that I would not see an eagle that day, as we had left their habitat behind.

———

Jerry and I were on our way to the surgical center where I was to have my sixth colonoscopy in about that many years. Both my parents died at young ages from colon cancer, and having this procedure on a regular basis saves me from following their fate. I am extremely grateful for it; however, the two-day medication preparation and fasting for the test always leaves me ill, weak and shaky, as it is complicated by other diseases that I have.

I thought about how loss and grief are cloaked in wisdom.

The night before, I had laid awake, thinking of the difficult last three years following the death of our beloved seventeen-year-old to suicide. It had been as if I were communing with memories too many to count. Briefly, I re-experienced the immediate horror and inconsolable sorrow at his death, which was now such a familiar, integrated part of my life. Especially at night when I can't sleep, grief is there like a hidden presence, teaching me things and revealing where true strength lies. I thought about how loss and grief are cloaked in wisdom, and I reflected ruefully that I had never wanted to be this wise.

The price I have paid is too high, the pain too deep, yet there it is—the gift that all who lose loved ones are given: the clarity to understand in our bones what is important in life. I learned to say yes to this blessing, but it was a fierce and wrenching assent. It finally evolved into a knowing spiritual confidence that did not take the grief away but rather walked with it, like night and morning overlapping in the river valley.

Earlier, as I kept my vigil and sat up in bed, carefully taking a small sip of water, I mused about the ministry work that has come to me as a result of Mic's death. Through Dr. Richard Johnson's newsletter from the Association for Lifelong Adult Ministry in St. Louis, I learned to define this as "love work" that all human beings are called to do all of our lives. I learned that we do not find a ministry; a ministry finds us. I could not, in my wildest dreams, have imagined being able to recover from the death of our son, much less help others to recover from their similar loss, but that is exactly what I had been called to do.

I have found another great blessing of grief in my very limitations. Because of my physical disabilities, I am limited in physical energy and the ability to reach out. Yet, my spiritual energy has expanded and awakened with such width, depth and breadth that it is nothing short of a miracle. My ego, while still present, has taken a back seat to my desire to help others, and I find (as do others whose ministry rises out of tragedy) that there is a new vulnerability in me that recognizes the need for dependence upon God.

The week our Web site's new message board for the survivors of a loved one's suicide was operational, I had a dream. I dreamt of being in a church with row upon row of expressionless, rigid people in pews. We were all asked to rise from our pews, hold hands, form a giant, living circle around the empty pews—which we did. For several days, the dream stayed vividly in my memory as I thought of the sheer happiness on the faces of all the people in the circle. On the Web, I posted my thoughts about the dream: "What a powerful message it would be for us to rise from our separateness and isolation and merge into the great community of God. A community is not a community without people, and there is much comfort that needs to be given and received. This is a calling extended to each of us."

Jean Vanier, the beloved founder of the *L'Arche* communities, said in an interview that the aim of his ministry is not to change the world, "but to create little places...where love is possible." He also said, "Real community is painful. I've been doing this for thirty-eight years and this is what I've learned... a community is a place of pain." As a person with a new ministry, those words actually comforted me, because they are realistic while still being affirming.

—

I am a prolific quote collector, but I only have one stuck above my computer screen on a Post-It note. It reads, *Let go and let God.* I find this saying from Alcoholics Anonymous applies not only to my trust and dependence upon God to work through me, but also to my relationship with the partners who arrive to assist and walk the journey with me. I have to admit that there was a time when I was uptight about this, because my companions hadn't arrived yet and I couldn't make them appear. I was doing my part and taking initiative (which I am a big believer in) but on its own, this is not enough. I had to learn the spirituality of waiting and patience—another great, ongoing lesson for those who mourn.

> *Eventually, the universe seemed to gather the mentors, colleagues, facilitators and community members I needed.*

Eventually, one by one, the universe seemed to gather the mentors, colleagues, facilitators and community members I needed. I stood by in amazement. My close friend and one of our site facilitators recently posted an important message about human relationships and ministry work. She said that humans often seek to be understood first rather than seeking to understand others; that we listen with the intent to reply, preoccupied with what we will say as we filter other people's thoughts through our own experience. Her comments reminded me that while I am finding my way on this lifetime journey called grief, my experiences and ways of finding comfort may not necessarily be those of others. I must remind myself to listen to other people's stories for the sake of extending nurturing listening, not to project my own tragedy into theirs.

—

That night in the truck, while suffering from a reaction to another dose of the necessary medication before my procedure the next morning, thoughts continued to click through my mind one after another, as if in a kaleidoscope or children's viewmaster.

Click... Here are the first, second and third year anniversaries of our son's death.

Click-click... Here are the faces of family and friends who walked the journey with us.

Click-click-click... Here are the three books I wrote and the two outreach Web sites Jerry and I established.

As I found my voice, studied, became educated in suicide and depression and began the work that shapes my life to this day, I found that at last I had grown spacious enough inside to have room for the grief, rather than having it consume my every waking thought. It was as if I went from living in one vast chamber of tears to dwelling in an inner space of countless rooms that never cease construction. When Jesus says that the Father prepares many mansions for us, to me this is a metaphor for the phenomenon of maturing spiritually as grief grows up.

I've put considerable reflection into the dynamics of my work, writing and ministry, and while first and foremost it is a labor of love, it is also not without struggle—despite all the blessings and lessons I've learned and tried to take to heart. I remember the phrase "To whom much has been given, much is expected" only too well...and some days, I feel too used up to rise to the occasion. Or worse still, I have made mistakes, said the wrong thing, read a person wrong or over-reacted to something. When these human limitations present themselves and I feel momentarily discouraged, I have to remind myself that all human beings have strengths and weaknesses and that my ministry is no different.

However, my commitment to my work seems to ebb and flow regularly with a rhythmic sense of spiritual momentum that is self-renewing and not dependent upon my mood of the day. I also remember that for some people's situations, grief and pain are too raw, too new, too deep for human words. It is important for me to realize that I am doing God's work, not Joni's work. Therefore, when I run out of ways to extend comfort, I can relinquish and prayerfully surrender the person to God's care while still offering my presence. However imperfect and human that may be, it is still a gift.

It always comes down to faith. We talk a lot about faith on our Web site, because it is the one, lone thing that is there when the bottom falls out for people. It is difficult sometimes to see people wrestle with it, but that is an important, vital part of the grief journey. We try to support and embrace that doubt, rather than offering answers, yet at the same time we are gently there with consistent words of hope and inspiration.

You are born and resurrected into a new faith within the fragile shell of what was your broken heart.

I am reminded of how, when a chick is about to hatch out of an egg, it has to do a lot of work. First, its tiny beak manages to poke a hole in the egg, and sometimes that is all you can see as you hear the peeping within the egg. It's like the chick is saying, *"Get me out of here, I'm worn out and new to this, break the shell for me and release me."* In my ministry work, I would like to be able to break the shell of grief for people. It's a good thing I cannot, however. Because then the people I work with would not learn to find their own strength and develop their own endurance that their journey requires. When the chick finally does emerge from the egg, it lies there within its broken shell, all spent and wet, but free at last. In a short time, it gathers itself, rises on its funny, large feet and starts pecking around for food.

To me, the faith process is like that for grieving people. You are born and resurrected into a new faith within the fragile shell of what was your broken heart.

When I think of all the paradoxical blessings grief has brought to me, I know my journey has been nothing short of extraordinary. I can't wrap my mind around it and don't try to. Instead, my life's mission is to live life simply and mindfully one day at a time and to be an authentic spiritual voice of comfort and insight as much as I can. This privilege can and does overwhelm me at times, but I experience the reality of it nonetheless. Gratitude sweeps through me for having survived the suicide of our son, and I have come to realize and affirm the most important revelation God blesses us with: that we are meant to flourish—not *despite* but *because of* the sorrow we bear. To allow our lives to flourish—even in our sorrow—honors our loved ones who have died and lifts the bearer of sorrow like an eagle riding the winds, high above and beyond that which has shattered our lives, hopes and dreams.

Believing in the blessings of grief is a radical concept that I would not have been open to accepting during that first difficult year. To be receptive to this idea would have seemed an absurd betrayal of the loss of our son. But now I know that all our deceased loved ones want us to have this blessing as we recreate meaningful lives.

As my husband and I motored through the river valley and morning and night seemed to overlap and co-exist at the same time, it struck me that grief and its blessings are like that as well. Through faith and our instincts, we can recognize the truth of this and find peace, purpose and comfort.

I greatly needed that comfort the next day at my medical procedure. As my kind doctor inserted the sedation medication into my I.V. and humorously asked if I would like a little nap, I murmured a grateful yes. As I drifted off, I smiled secretly, because right above me as I laid on the surgical gurney, taped to the ceiling, was a magnificent poster of a soaring eagle.

"God Helps Those Who Let Him"

by Michael Leach

Vickie and I had been married a year and were living comfortably in a Greenwich Village studio not much larger than a hot tub. Neither of us made a lot of money, but we always had enough and a little bit more. Life in the studio was warm and good.

But I knew I had to get ahead or we'd never be able to afford a space that was big enough for the family we wanted to grow. The thought of not having enough in the future began to chill my mind like a draft coming through a crack in a window.

"It's okay," Vickie assured me. "We have each other, that's all we need. My parents raised five of us on very little. We'll be fine. God is taking care of us."

"You're the most grateful person I've ever known."

"God gave me a miracle. How can I not be grateful?"

Vickie had fallen on a glass toy when she was a baby. It shattered and blinded her right eye. The good eye was hazel and specked with green, the blind one a milky blue. When we first met and fell in love she told me how she grew up feeling like a freak. "When the kids played games I always had to be the bad guy or the monster. People still look at me and recoil. All I've ever wanted is to look like everybody else and find my prince."

She was so beautiful. And when I said so, she knew I meant it.

Shortly after we married the blind eye got sick. It had to be removed before it affected the sight in the good eye. Vickie had two operations. A specialist painted an artificial eye that perfectly matched the hazel one specked with green. In her eyes she now looked like everybody else. In mine she was as beautiful as ever. Vickie glowed with gratitude as easily and often as the sun radiates light.

In her eyes she now looked like everybody else. In mine she was as beautiful as ever.

She would lay her head on my chest and say, "This is the way I always dreamed it would be."

"Yes," I'd agree. "It's perfect."

"Tell me how it's going to be."

"It will always be like this. But one day we'll live in a little white house with a white picket fence, with two kids as beautiful as you, and a shaggy dog we'll call Heathcliffe."

"Skip the dog. Talk about the kids."

"We'll love them, all the time, and we'll play with them and comfort them when they're sad. You'll help them with their homework, and I'll teach them how to swim. In the fall we'll rake leaves into mountains of gold and throw them on you and you'll laugh. In the winter we'll all make snowmen and give them great big smiles."

"Like the movie *Christmas in Connecticut?*"

"Better."

Our imaginations danced like children through a pile of leaves.

But I kept on thinking, how will we ever be able to afford it?

———

When I had left the Catholic priesthood the previous year to marry, I decided to become a book editor. But the only job I could land with no experience was writing religious education materials for the Episcopal Church. So without being asked I began to make proposals for books, like the one from a priest named Richard Bolles who wrote sermons for a series I edited called "Selected Sermons." Dick was working on a job-hunting guide for people leaving the ministry called *What Color Is Your Parachute?* But the publisher did not think it would have a big enough market and turned it down.

At the end of my first year of work a recession hit hard and a lot of people lost their jobs. I was grateful to keep mine, but I continued to be afraid that our dream of how it was going to be would always be a dream. So I answered a blind ad for an editor of Catholic religious education magazines in the Midwest. I still wanted to do books, but I knew we could buy a house with a white picket fence in Ohio for half the price of one in New York.

I never expected the phone call inviting me to fly out for an interview.

Or the next one inviting Vickie and me to come down for a weekend.

The job was mine.

Two of the people I'd be working with, Pete and John, were our age and just starting their families. Vickie and I would have instant friends. They showed us two-bedroom townhouses with rents not much higher than our studio in New York! We signed a lease on a brand new one. I'd start the job in six weeks. The way it was going to be was going to be *soon*.

The dream had turned to nightmare.

Back in New York Vickie and I told our bosses and our landlord. Packing was easy; all we had was a few books and records and clothes. A week before we were to go, Vickie told me she was pregnant. We embraced for a long time.

The next day my new friend Pete called. He was at La Guardia. "I have to see you. Right away."

I took a cab to the airport.

Over coffee Pete warned, "Mike, don't come."

"What do you mean? I start next week."

"There's not going to be a job. The company has new ownership. Things have changed. For all of us."

"You're kidding."

He wasn't. The dream had turned to nightmare.

Humbly, we asked our landlord if we could stay in the studio. We could, but at a much higher rent.

Vickie got her job back but would give birth in nine months. Where would we put the baby?

I approached my former boss with apprehension and told him what happened. He was delighted. He gave me my job back, and a raise. We could afford to stay in the studio until we ran out of room.

Before Chris was born we moved to an affordable one-bedroom apartment in New Jersey. I joked that we were like Joseph and Mary who had to flee into Egypt. Vickie stood on the balcony facing the sunrise and said, "This is perfect!"

—

I loved lifting our new baby high in the air and making him laugh. I marveled at how he knew I would never drop him, never let him fall. I wrote a sermon for the "Selected Sermons" series on how God was like a father who throws us high in the air and always catches us, how we need to trust God and, like children, laugh and say, "Do it again! Do it again!"

Those were nice words, but now I was worrying that I'd never make enough money to give our son a bedroom of his own. Worse, I looked around and saw people who I didn't think were as smart as I was or worked as hard as I did but who had things we didn't have.

When Vickie got pregnant with Jeff six months after Chris was born, she was grateful. But I was anxious. What would I do? How would I provide?

Vickie confronted me. "You have to stop this! Be grateful for what we have! We have each other!"

Ice in my face couldn't have wakened me faster. I was ignoring the gifts in front of me in favor of fear and jeopardizing our life together because of disappointment in not being somebody else. We embraced for a long time. I prayed hard.

For some reason I remembered a notice that had been on the bulletin board at work. The national Church owned a house in Connecticut that they rented to Episcopal priests. I was sure I didn't qualify, and, truth is, I hardly knew where Connecticut was. But the next day I went to the treasurer and asked about it.

To us it was the biggest, grandest, most wonderful home we had ever seen.

"No one else has asked," he said, "and you qualify as a priest in my book. The house is yours if you want it."

Connecticut turned out to be a paradise of trees along the shoreline of Long Island Sound. The house was a little ranch with three small bedrooms and a stonewall fence near the edge of town. To us it was the biggest, grandest, most wonderful home we had ever seen. And the rent was exactly what we had been paying for the studio in Manhattan.

Jeff was born ten days before our first Christmas in Connecticut. It was just like I said it was going to be. It was the best Christmas we ever had!

You might think this is the end of the story but it isn't.

—

I rode the New Haven railroad to the city with my neighbor Jack, a good man who helped me assemble Christmas toys and lent us his second car when ours broke down. He taught me how to fold the *New York Times* down into a square like the other commuters so I wouldn't have to read the *New York Post*. Life was good but somehow I still felt like a *New York Post* kind of guy, a fraud who would be exposed if the stock-brokers and bankers I imagined filled the rest of the train really knew how I got to sit next to them.

That spring the publisher asked me to be the director of a new department. I was grateful but also took the opportunity to remind him that what I really wanted was to be a book editor. He said I could do both if I could pull it off, and he offered me another raise.

I worked hard and became vice president of the company three years later. I also wrote a book, edited a magazine, ran a book club, and without missing a beat taught our sons to swim, turned leaves into mountains of gold in the fall, and made snowmen who smiled in December. The Church sold us our perfect little house at an affordable price. How could life get any better?

So I began to worry how we'd ever pay for college in ten years. And wondered if the house would be big enough when the kids were in high school.

Then something happened.

A dear friend, robust and larger than life, withered away from cancer.

His death struck me like the words of truth Vickie spoke to me five years earlier. All of a sudden he was here, and just as suddenly he was gone.

I was sitting in my office, sad and stunned. Like Alfie, I asked myself, "What's it all about?" I was helping authors with words that changed other people's lives but not my own. I looked over to my bookshelf. "Read a book for yourself," a voice said to me. "Learn something that will help you, just like you did when you read for spiritual nourishment in the seminary."

My eyes lit on a book called *Dialogues in Metapsychiatry*, written by a psychiatrist named Thomas Hora. Another editor had acquired it. I remembered his saying, "This is far out but really good." I thought, that's just what I need.

I opened the book and read: "All problems are psychological but all solutions are spiritual." I kept reading.

—

A week later I called the author, who had a practice in the city, and asked to meet him. He invited me to his office. I told myself I wanted to see him just to find out if he was the real thing. In truth, I was hoping he was the real thing.

He was.

Dr. Hora called his patients "students." Among them were

some prominent writers of spiritual books. I started to realize that getting the words right doesn't mean we always get our lives right. I attended Dr. Hora's group sessions on Wednesday nights for three years and began to understand that I didn't have to get ahead (of whom?) or even climb a ladder to God (where I already lived and moved and had my being). I recognized that blessings were bursting into my life all the time – despite my efforts, not because of them.

> Dr. Hora reminded me of truths that were as close to me as breathing but that I had buried like children under a pile of leaves.

Dr. Hora said that "we work for money but live for God." He helped me to realize that it made no sense to strive to be like everyone else, that I was already made in the image and likeness of God. What could be more beautiful than to "glow for God" on the spot where I was standing? Dr. Hora reminded me of truths that were as close to me as breathing but that I had buried like children under a pile of leaves.

Moments of clarity brought peace, gratitude and assurance. I knew that I would later hide these glimpses of light under a bushel of unawareness, but I could never lose them. Dr. Hora used to joke that it's easy to be enlightened, it's just hard to be interested in enlightenment. One of his principles was, "God helps those who let him." I've never exactly understood what that means, but I do know it has everything to do with this story, and the ongoing story of my life.

God is blessing me all the time, whether I know it or not. I don't have to influence anyone or interfere with anything. I need only see the Love and Intelligence that is already here.

Funny thing: Vickie has always seemed to know that without needing words. When she received the gift of a new eye, she "got it," knew it, then and there. Others of us need God to "do it again," which is, of course, what God keeps doing all the time.

—

Dr. Hora passed away in 1995. A student asked him as he lay dying, "What's the one thing you'd like us all to know?"

"Just be grateful," he answered.

It's more than thirty years since Vickie and I snuggled in our Greenwich Village studio that was as warm and cozy as a hot tub. We now live in a bigger house, our boys have grown into men, and Vickie makes sure we are both aware of our blessings all the time.

Sure, my life can still go from a musical to a horror flick to the sweet ending of *The Wizard of Oz* all in a day, but I know now more than ever that God's grace connects every dot, every fall, every rising. Vickie would not have become the most grateful person I've ever known without losing her eye. Christmas in Connecticut would never have happened without the loss of Ohio. The rediscovery of my spiritual roots was at one with the loss of a friend. And the passing of a teacher reminded me again that life's purest blessing is simply to live with gratitude on the spot where we're standing.

Can enlightenment be as simple—and difficult—as turning on the switch in a dark room? Is living in the world just as effortless—and challenging—as the principle, "God helps those who let him"? Is the sum of our life a single blessing that transforms loss, or a series of blessings, big and small, that invite us to "glow for God" once and for all?

You may think this story is over, but it isn't.

Afterword

or Christians of all denominations, sorrow and loss are mitigated by our belief in resurrection. This is not easy for us to explain, because the last thing we want to communicate is that bad things somehow become good (or even no longer quite so bad).

Our starting point for this belief is the passion and death of Jesus of Nazareth. There's not much worse that can happen to a human being than what happened to Jesus (and his mother and friends). He was unjustly accused, tortured and humiliated, abandoned by almost all of his followers. Finally, he died one of the most terrible deaths imaginable.

Those who murdered him would have preferred to say he was executed as a common criminal, but one of the key points in the gospels is that Jesus was completely innocent. He did nothing to deserve what happened to him, yet he was killed anyway—hung naked on a tree, in front of his mother, between two thieves.

The crucifixion was a bad thing. It should not have happened. If we could go back in time, we would stop it if we could.

Yet we believe that somehow this very bad thing led to the greatest blessing the world has ever received. Through the power of God, Jesus was raised from the dead. And like the beloved disciple when he looked inside the empty tomb, we Christians believe this with all our hearts, even though we do "not yet understand."

The implications of the resurrection are staggering: Our relationship with God has been permanently repaired; our sins have been forgiven; we have been reconciled with one another; we have been promised eternal life.

All these blessings flowed from the death of Jesus. The resurrection transformed the crucifixion into something else, something that was the instrument of our salvation, even though we wish Jesus had not suffered it. We Christians call this miracle the Paschal Mystery, and we feel that the same process of "life out of death" continues in each of our lives.

Bad things happen. They happen to good people. But God offers blessings that transform our sorrow and loss, if we let them.

Like the blessings whose stories appear in this book.

About the Contributors

Father James Stephen (Jeffrey) Behrens, OCSO, is an oblate at the Monastery of the Holy Spirit in Conyers, Georgia, and a priest of the Archdiocese of Newark, New Jersey. He is the author of *Grace Is Everywhere* and *Memories of Grace*.

Alice Camille is a religious educator and the author of *Invitation to Catholicism, The Rosary* and *Seven Last Words*.

Kass Dotterweich is the editor of *Catechist* magazine and the author of *25 Stories for Sharing Faith with Teens*.

Father Patrick Hannon, CSC, is the principal and a teacher of literature at Notre Dame High School in Niles, Illinois.

Helen Lambin is a retired college administrator and the author of *The Death of a Husband* and *From Grief to Grace*.

Michael Leach is the publisher of Orbis Books and the co-author of *I Like Being Catholic* and *I Like Being Married*.

Terry Nelson-Johnson is the director of faith formation at Old St. Patrick's Church in Chicago and a lecturer and writer on youth sexuality.

Robert Raccuglia is the director of the Cenacle Retreat and Conference Center in Chicago and the former executive director of Serra International.

Patrick T. Reardon is a reporter for the *Chicago Tribune* and the author of *Daily Meditations (with Scripture) for Busy Dads* and *Starting Out: Reflections for Young People*.

Joyce Rupp, OSM, is a speaker and writer and the author

of *Praying Our Goodbyes, The Cup of Our Life,* and *The Cosmic Dance.*

Joni Woelfel is a writer for the *National Catholic Reporter* and other publications and the author of *The Light Within, Tall in Spirit,* and *Meditations for Survivors of Suicide.*

Vinita Hampton Wright is an editor for Loyola Press and the author of the novel *Velma Still Cooks in Leeway,* the novella *The Winter Seeking,* and the nonfiction book *Simple Acts of Moving Forward.*

Acknowledgments

You cannot compile a collection of great original stories unless you know a lot of great storytellers. Fortunately, I do.

Thanks to James (Jeff) Behrens, Alice Camille, Kass Dotterweich, Pat Hannon, Helen Lambin, Mike Leach, Terry Nelson-Johnson, Bob Raccuglia, Pat Reardon, Joyce Rupp, Joni Woelfel and Vinita Wright—first for being such good friends and colleagues and secondly for sharing their stories with me and with you.

I also want to thank Matthew, Mark, Luke, John and the billions of Christians over the centuries since the birth of Jesus who have kept alive the story of the Paschal Mystery. They have reminded us of this central truth of Christianity: God does not bring us bad things; God sends us the blessings that can transform our sorrows or loss, if—as Mike Leach puts it—we but let him.

And finally to you, dear reader, I offer my sincere appreciation. For a book is truly complete only when someone has read it from the beginning to the end.

If you enjoyed *Hidden Presence*, you might also like the award-winning book *Christmas Presence: Twelve Gifts That Were More Than They Seemed*, published by ACTA Publications. Included are twelve stories of Christmas gifts the authors received that revealed the presence of God to them in a special way. Contributors include James Behrens, Alice Camille, Kass Dotterweich, Patrick Hannon, Michael Leach, Patrick T. Reardon, Vinita Hampton Wright and five other great spiritual writers. *Christmas Presence* is published as a $17.95 hardcover with gift ribbon. It is available from booksellers or by calling 800-397-2282 or at www.actapublications.com.